FAITH AND RUIN
EXPLORING THE ABANDONED CHURCHES IN TEXAS

ADRIANA PEREZ

—
AMERICA
—
THROUGH
—
TIME

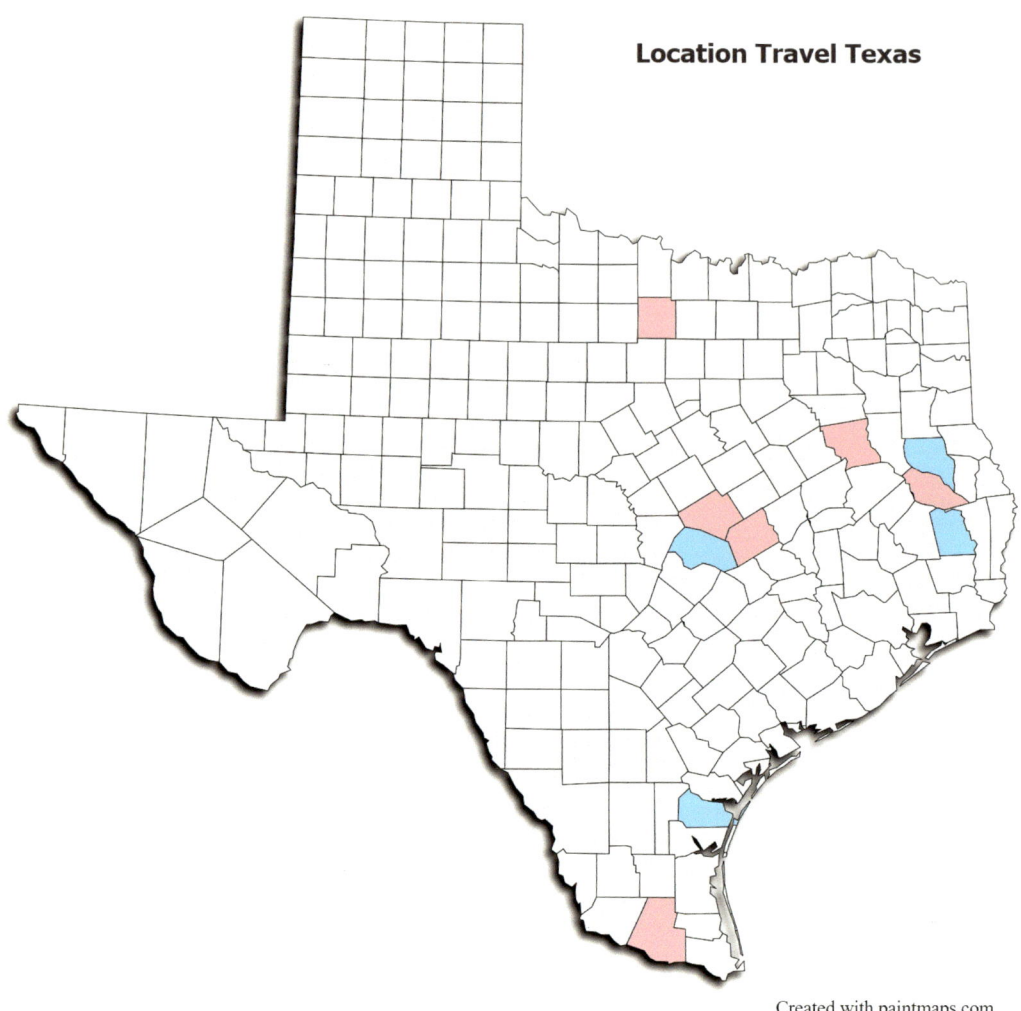

Location Travel Texas

Created with paintmaps.com

AMERICA THROUGH TIME®
An imprint of SUTTON PUBLISHING INC
www.through-time.com

First published 2025
Copyright © Adriana Perez 2025

ISBN 978-1-63499-529-0

Typeset in 10pt on13pt Sabon
Printed and bound in England

Contents

Introduction

Texas is a land where faith has shaped not just communities, but the very foundation of its identity. From the early Spanish missions to the vast array of churches dotting small towns and urban landscapes, religion has long been woven into the cultural fabric of the state. Yet, as Texas grows and changes, many of these sacred spaces are left behind—abandoned, crumbling, and forgotten. Their decay tells a story that goes beyond faded paint and broken pews. It speaks to the broader systemic and political issues that ripple through Texas and our nation today.

Faith and Ruin: Exploring the Abandoned Churches of Texas is not just a photographic exploration of these spaces; it is an examination of what their decline reveals about us. These churches once served as pillars of their communities—places of worship, refuge, and connection. Now, they stand as silent witnesses to shifting demographics, economic collapse, rural depopulation, environmental neglect, and the impact of policies that prioritize growth over preservation.

My name is Adriana Perez. I am a photographer, realtor, urban explorer, and someone who has always been drawn to the spaces that most people overlook. My journey into abandoned churches began with a camera and a question: What happened? As I travelled across Texas, capturing these enigmatic wonders, I realized this book was about more than just documenting these discarded places, it was about the histories of racial injustice, economic disparity, the erosion of small-town America, and the political decisions that have shaped these outcomes. This book combines photography, historical research, and personal reflection to tell their stories. Some churches have been repurposed, others ravaged by scrappers and squatters or demolished, and a few are being reclaimed by nature. Each image gives way to a deeper conversation about community, resilience, and the cost of neglect—both literal and metaphorical.

At its core, Faith and Ruin is about the people who once filled the now broken pews, the systems that failed them, and the possibilities for renewal.

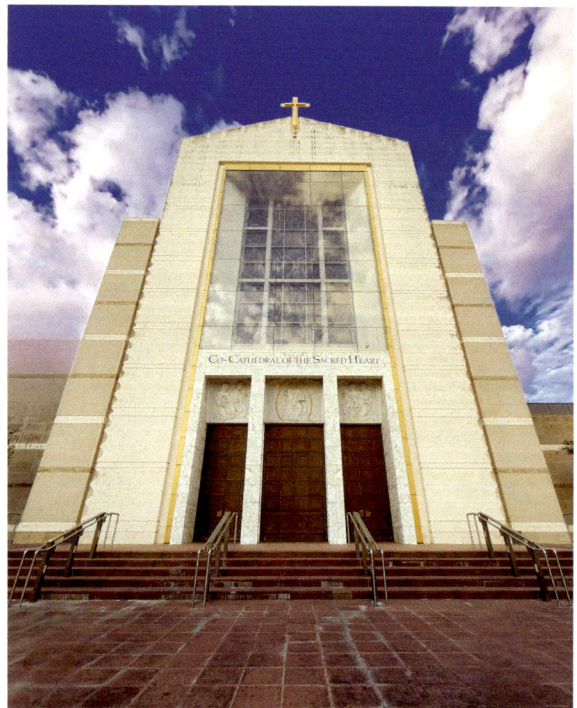

Co-Cathedral of the Sacred
Heart in Houston, Texas.

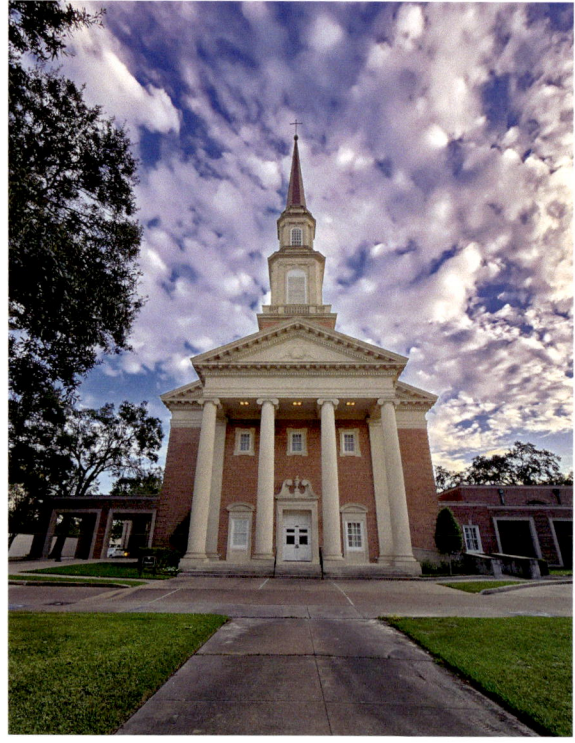

St. Lukes United Methodist
Church in Houston, Texas.

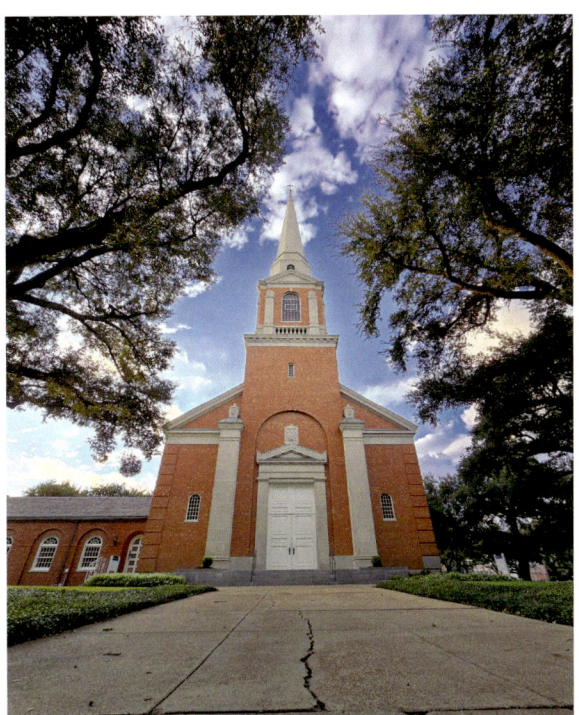

The First Presbyterian Church
in Houston, Texas.

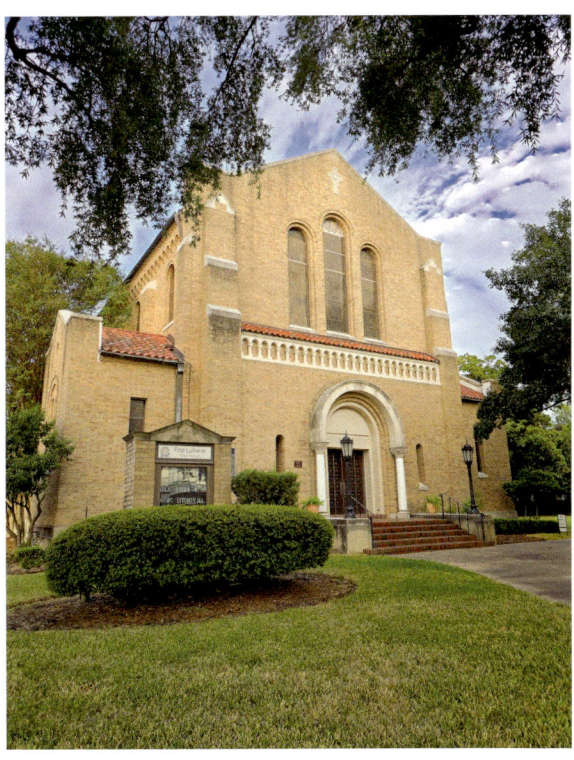

First Lutheran Church
in Houston, Texas.

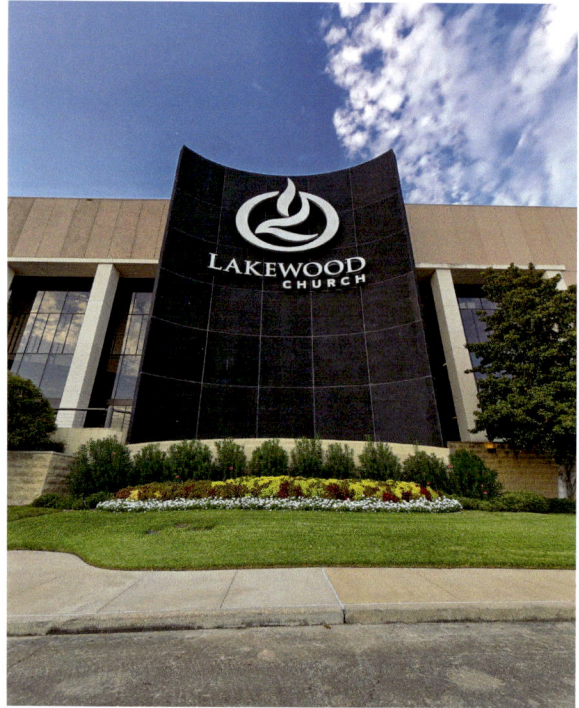

Lakewood Church in Houston, Texas.

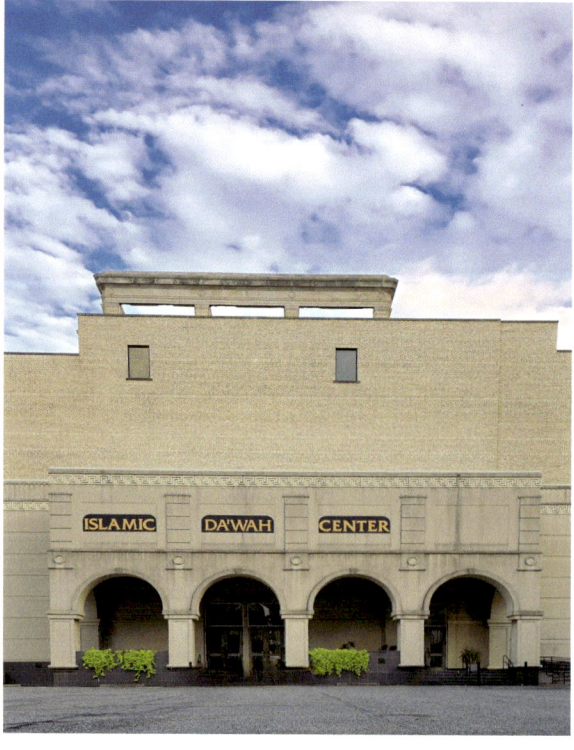

The Islamic Da'wah Center
in Houston, Texas.

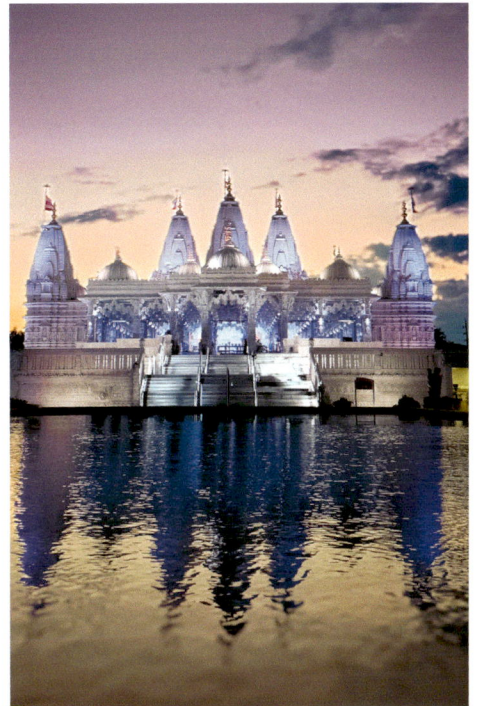

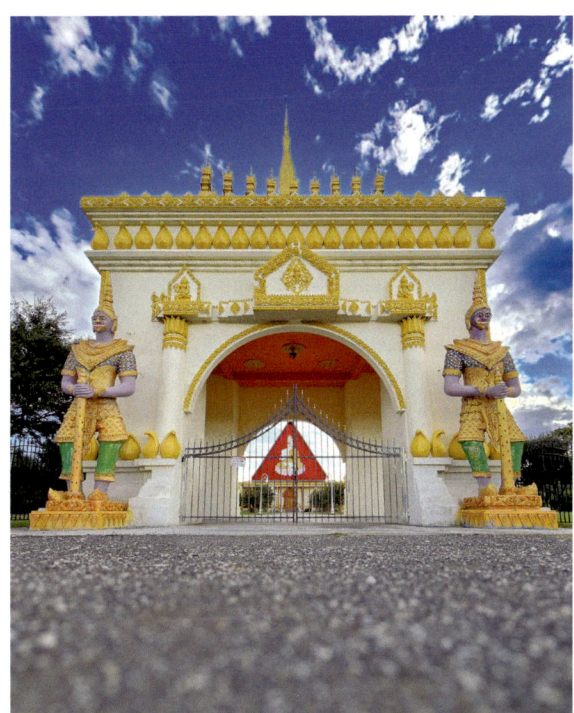

Above left: BAPS Shri
Swaminarayan Mandir, Houston.

Above right: The Wat Phouthasamakhy
Lao in Houston, Texas.

Right: Congregation Beth
Yeshurun in Houston, Texas.

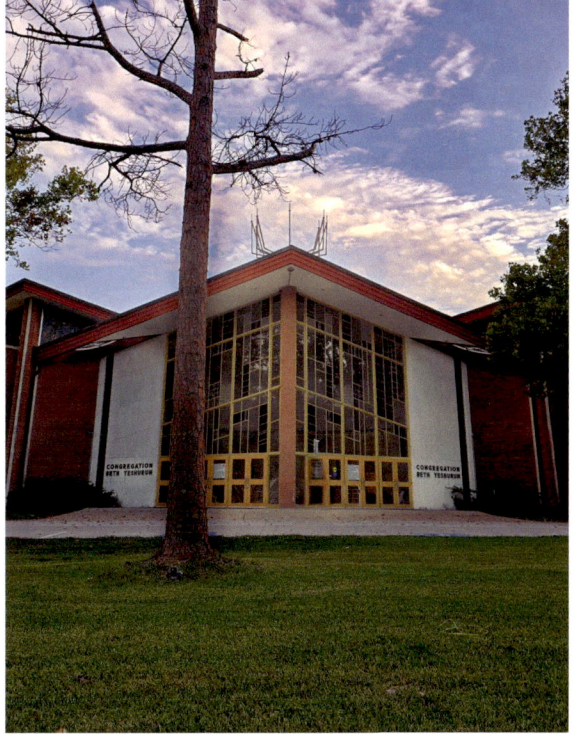

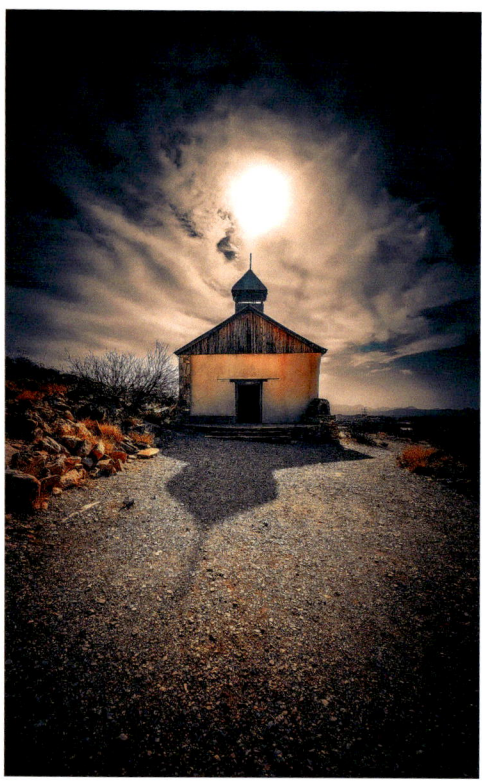

Left: In the remote expanse of Terlingua, Texas, near the majestic Big Bend, stands the Church of Santa Inez.

Below left: A quiet, snowy day envelops the rural heart of East Texas.

Below right: In Pearland, Texas, the Dharma Spring Temple holds a serene Buddha Sculpture.

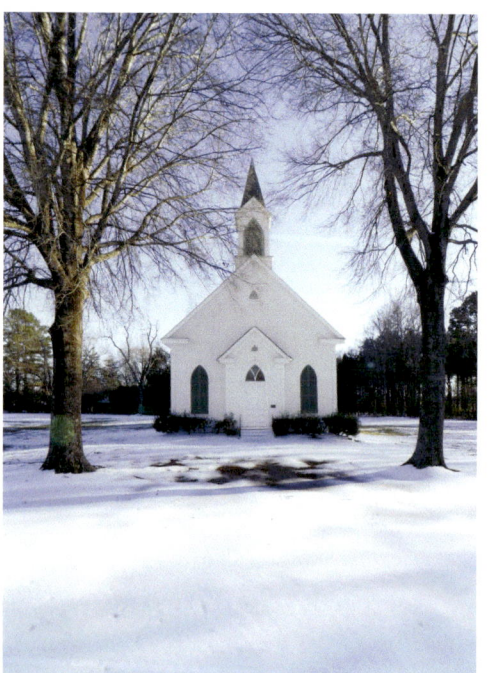

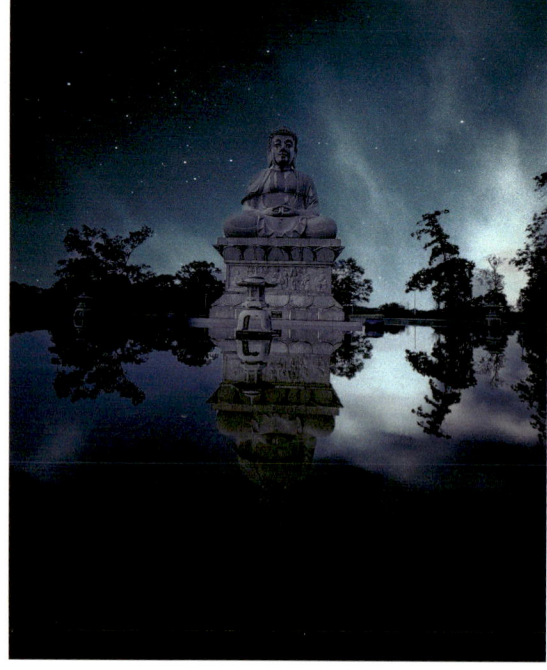

1

Unknown Church:
Jasper County, Jasper

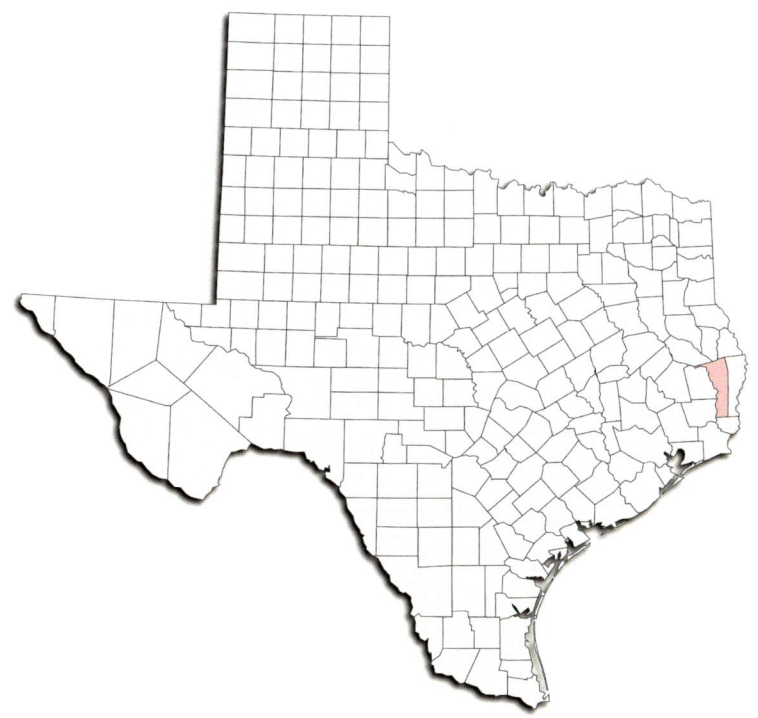

Created with paintmaps.com

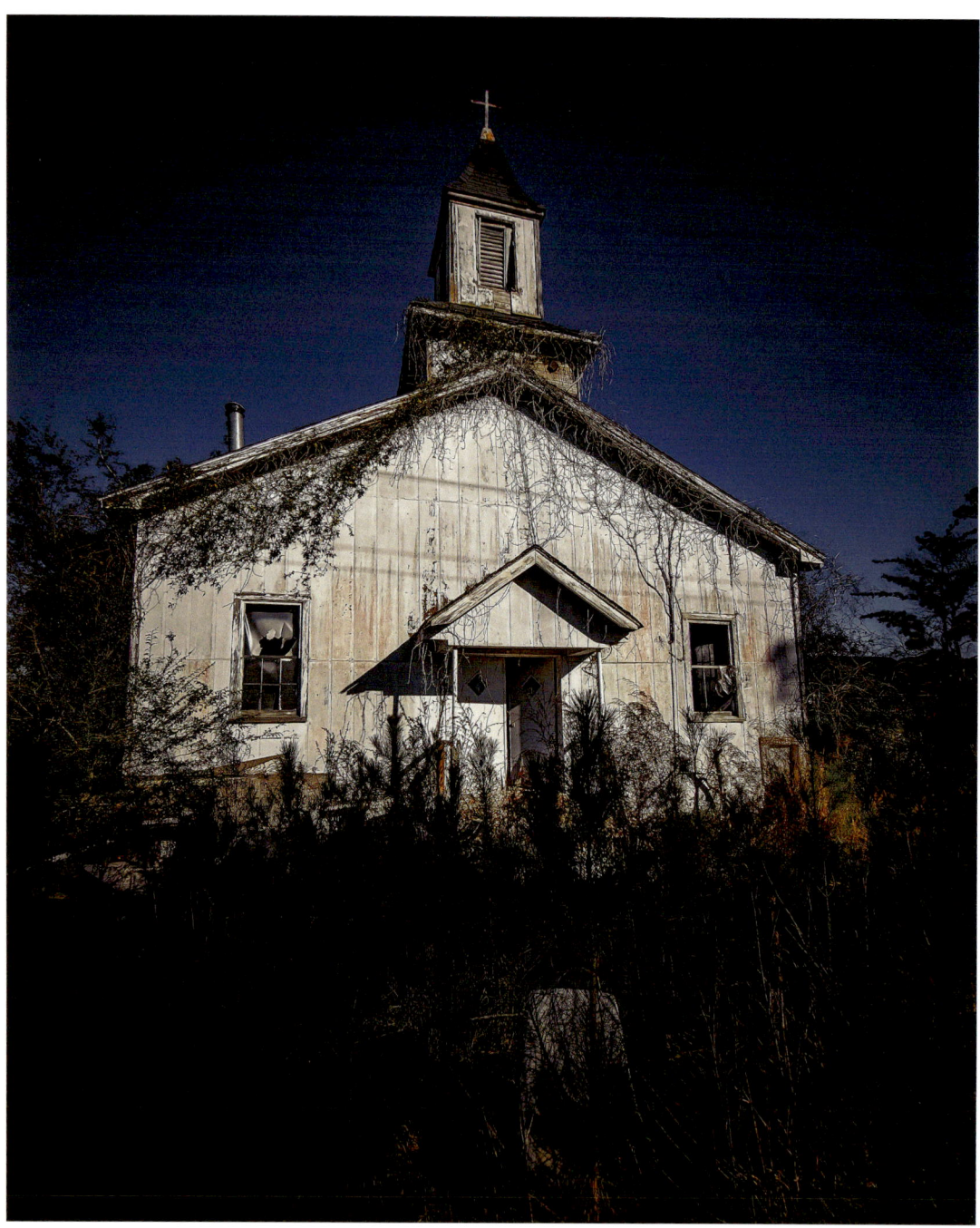

Exterior shot of Jasper church.

Jasper, Texas, settled around 1824 and incorporated in 1835, has a rich yet complex history of community, faith, and tragedy. Named after Revolutionary War hero Sergeant William Jasper, the town has evolved significantly over nearly two centuries. Jasper, like much of East Texas, has a history of segregation, racial violence, and Ku Klux Klan activity and is well known for the 1998 murder of James Byrd Jr. Churches in Jasper were crucial in advancing equality, providing spaces for organizing and protest, with pastors risking much to fight segregation and discrimination.

However, while the contributions of these churches to the community are well-documented, the history of the church pictured remains unknown, though its architectural style hints at the early days of Jasper's settlement.

The infamous murder of James Byrd, Jr., on June 7, 1998, is one of the most horrific hate crimes in recent American history. James Byrd, Jr., a forty-nine-year-old African American man, was brutally murdered by three white supremacists, who I will intentionally leave unnamed. The perpetrators offered Byrd a ride while walking home, but their intentions were far from friendly.

Byrd was taken to a remote area where he was beaten and then chained by his ankles to the back of a pickup truck. The men drove for approximately 3 miles, dragging Byrd along an asphalt road. The ordeal ended tragically when Byrd's body hit a culvert, severing his right arm and head. The remaining parts of his body were left in front of an African American cemetery to be found the following day.

The murder of James Byrd, Jr., stunned both Jasper, a town of about 7,600, and the nation. Known for its strong religious values and close-knit community, Jasper responded with grief, anger, and a resolve for justice. The three perpetrators were quickly arrested and charged with capital murder. The trials exposed the racial hatred behind the crime, revealing the men as members of a white supremacist gang, with one even having written a manifesto promoting racial violence.

Two of the men were convicted and sentenced to death. One was executed in 2011, and the other was executed in 2019. The third man involved, who was seen as less culpable, received a life sentence without the possibility of parole.

The murder of James Byrd, Jr., led to the 2001 Texas James Byrd Jr. Hate Crimes Act, which increased penalties for bias-motivated crimes. This law inspired the federal Matthew Shepard and James Byrd Jr. Hate Crimes Prevention Act of 2009 to expand hate crime definitions and resources. Jasper has since worked on racial reconciliation, with local leaders and groups promoting unity and commemorating Byrd's legacy. However, challenges persist. In 2012, amid political tensions, a newly elected city council, following a racially charged recall effort, dismissed Police Chief Rodney Pearson, leading to a discrimination lawsuit and a $831,000 settlement. The firing of Jasper's first black police chief exemplified ongoing struggles for racial equality and justice.

Like unextinguished embers, Jasper's past glows softly through its streets, and the haunting legacy of James Byrd, Jr., challenges us all to confront deep-rooted issues of racial inequality and injustice. While churches have played a pivotal role in the fight for civil rights, the enduring impact of past customs, laws, and beliefs has left minorities struggling. This ongoing struggle calls for a collective commitment to ensure that the lessons of history encourage genuine understanding, compromise, unity, and equality for all.

2

Mount Vernon African Methodist Episcopal Church: Anderson County, Palestine

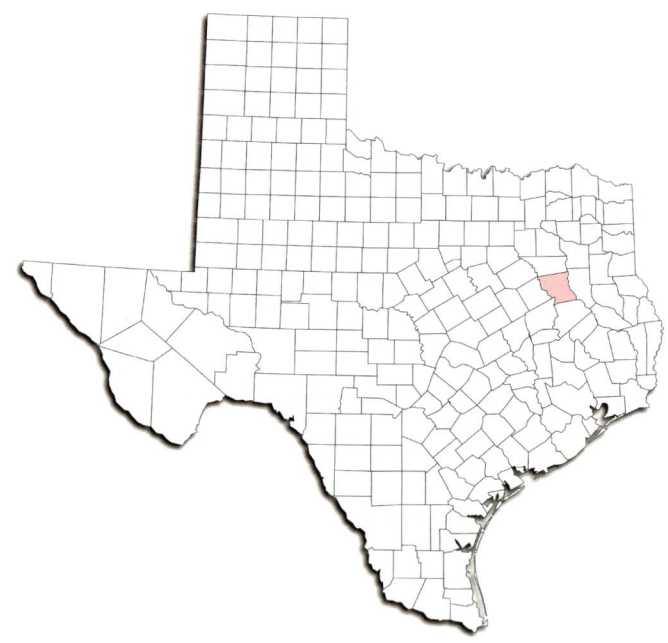

Created with paintmaps.con

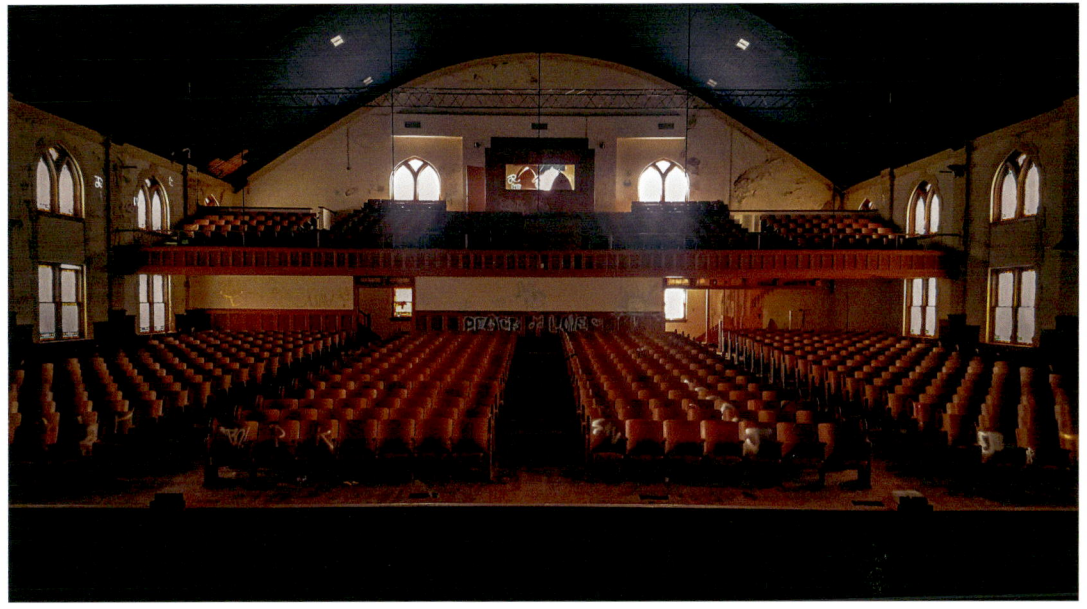

Main stage view of empty pews.

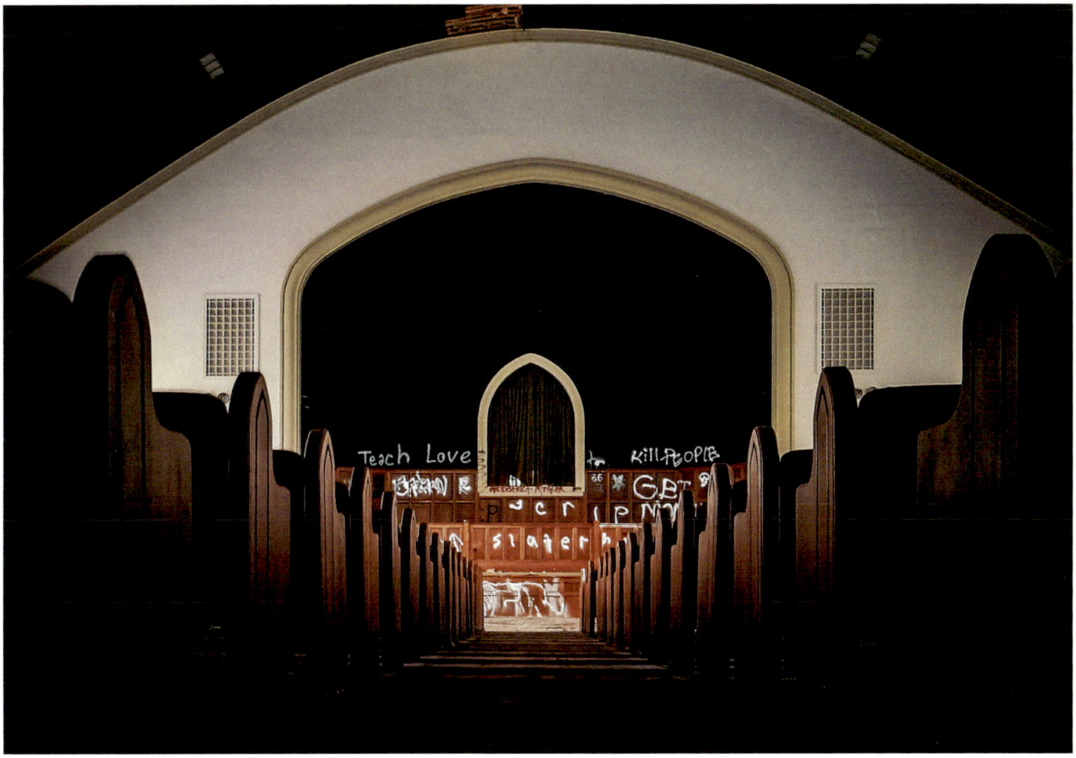

Center aisle of an abandoned church.

The city of Palestine, nestled in the pine trees and hills of East Texas, was founded in the early nineteenth century by Daniel Parker, who aptly named it to create a place of religious freedom. Over time, Palestine became a melting pot of cultures and religions, with Methodist, Baptist, Catholic, and Presbyterian churches playing key roles. In 1921, the African American community established Mount Vernon AME Church, founded by former slaves seeking spiritual freedom and a sense of belonging. Designed by James B. Roundtree, this Gothic-style church became a sanctuary and symbol of resilience, offering refuge, empowerment, and a community space for worship and support in a segregated society.

In 1968, Mount Vernon AME Church built a 100-unit complex, becoming the first in Palestine to introduce integrated low-income housing. This initiative demonstrated their commitment to helping the community's most vulnerable members and their mission of social justice and inclusiveness.

Redlining, a practice not just limited to Palestine, occurred nationwide and systematically denied African Americans and other non-white populations access to mortgages and homeownership by allowing banks, lenders, and government agencies to designate certain neighborhoods as high-risk based solely on racial composition, leading to loan denials, inflated interest rates, and disinvestment that perpetuated economic inequality and segregation for generations. As a result, these discriminatory policies created significant gaps in generational wealth among non-white communities, exacerbating economic disadvantages.

Completing the low-income housing complex in Palestine was a formidable challenge, especially in a community shaped by redlining, which complicated efforts to secure funding and support. While the Fair Housing Act passed in 1968 marked a significant step toward banning redlining, making it somewhat easier to access FHA loans that year, systemic disadvantages for people of color persisted. Despite initiatives designed to promote equitable access to housing, these efforts often fell short, perpetuating cycles of poverty. Mount Vernon AME Church remains a testament to the resilient spirit of the African American community, standing proudly despite historical challenges.

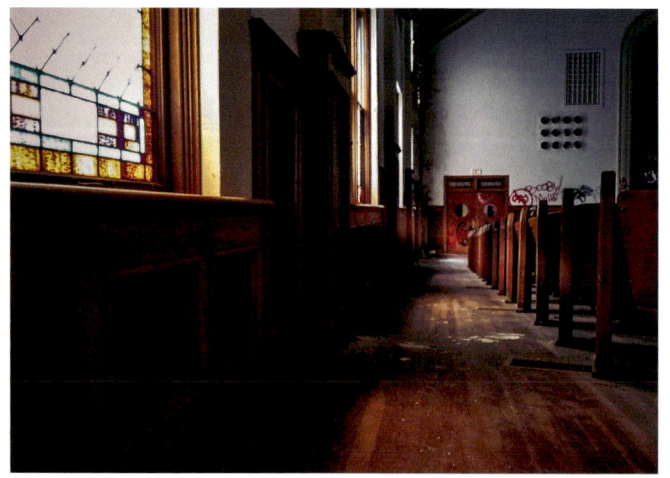 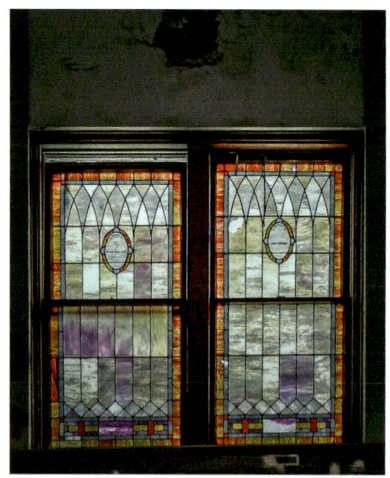

Above left: Faded stained-glass remnants.

Above right: Close-up of stained-glass details.

Mount Vernon itself is a sight to behold! Its stained-glass windows and weathered steeples enhance the church's unassuming architecture. The high curved ceiling, painted in a striking blue hue, commands attention. The second-floor viewing balcony has its own set of pews, which were undoubtedly the best seats in the house.

Unfortunately, during my visit, some parts of the church showed signs of severe neglect and were plagued by mold due to the lack of maintenance, which exposed them to the elements. Squatters, scrappers, and taggers have also contributed to the deterioration of the building.

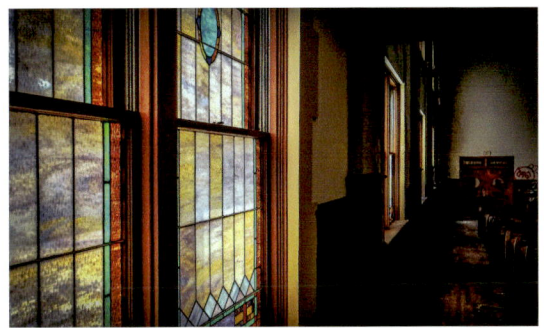 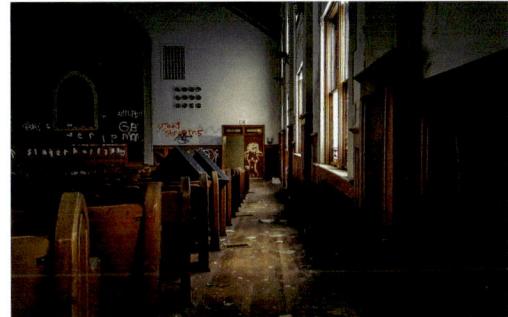

Above left: Cracked, faded stained-glass windows.

Above right: Vandalized rightmost aisle.

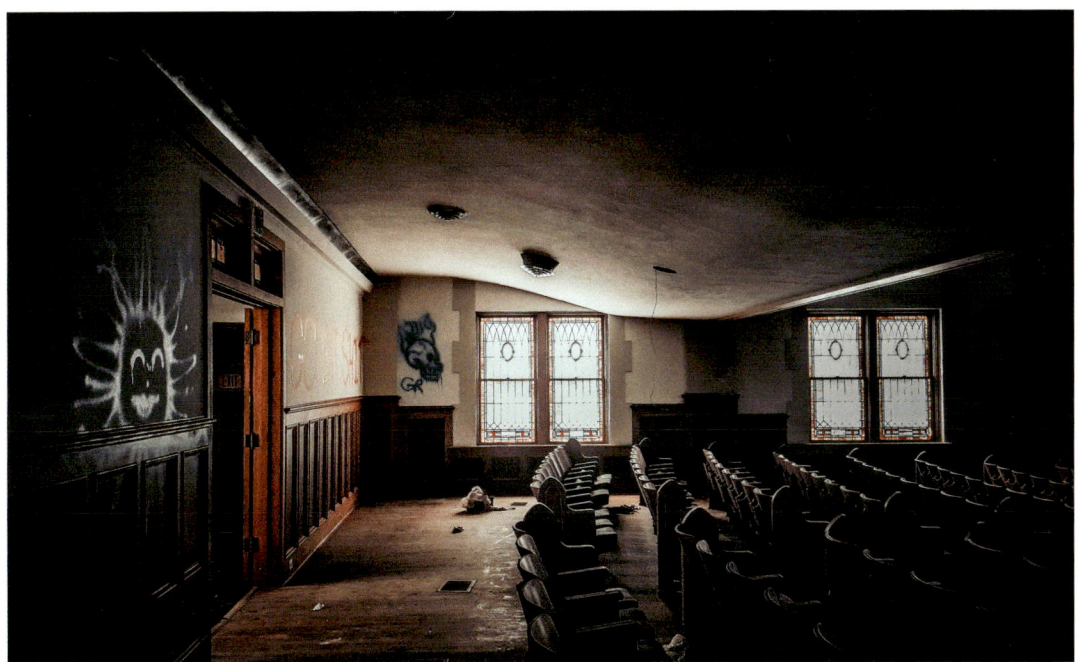

Vandalized upper deck view.

Like many historic landmarks, graffiti defaces the walls, valuable materials have been stripped, and intentional damage mars the interior and exterior. Despite this, the church's dilapidated walls possess a haunting beauty. Nature is reclaiming the space, with vines creeping through floor cracks and sunlight dancing on moss-covered walls, creating an eerie yet captivating atmosphere.

In 2023, the community rallied to preserve Mount Vernon AME Church, securing a $75,000 grant for repairs. The renovation promises to restore the old structure and protect it from further damage . This revival brings hope and optimism, reminding us that despite adversity, faith and perseverance can lead to a brighter future for generations to come.

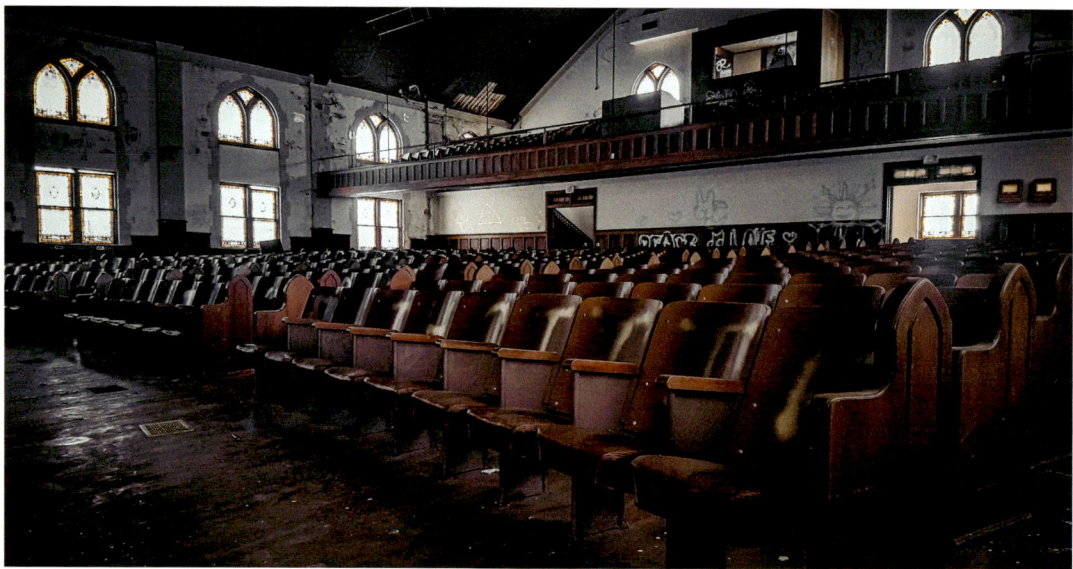

View of main floor seating, upper deck seating, and projector room.

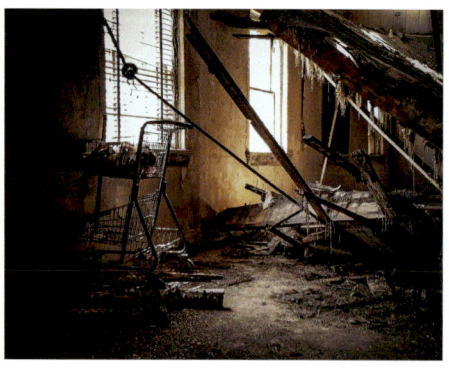

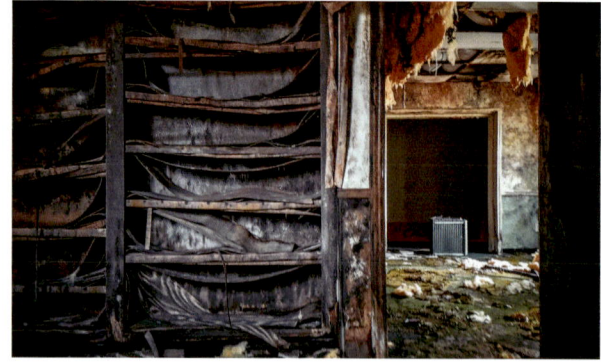

Signs of squatters and damage.

Decaying bookshelf in office.

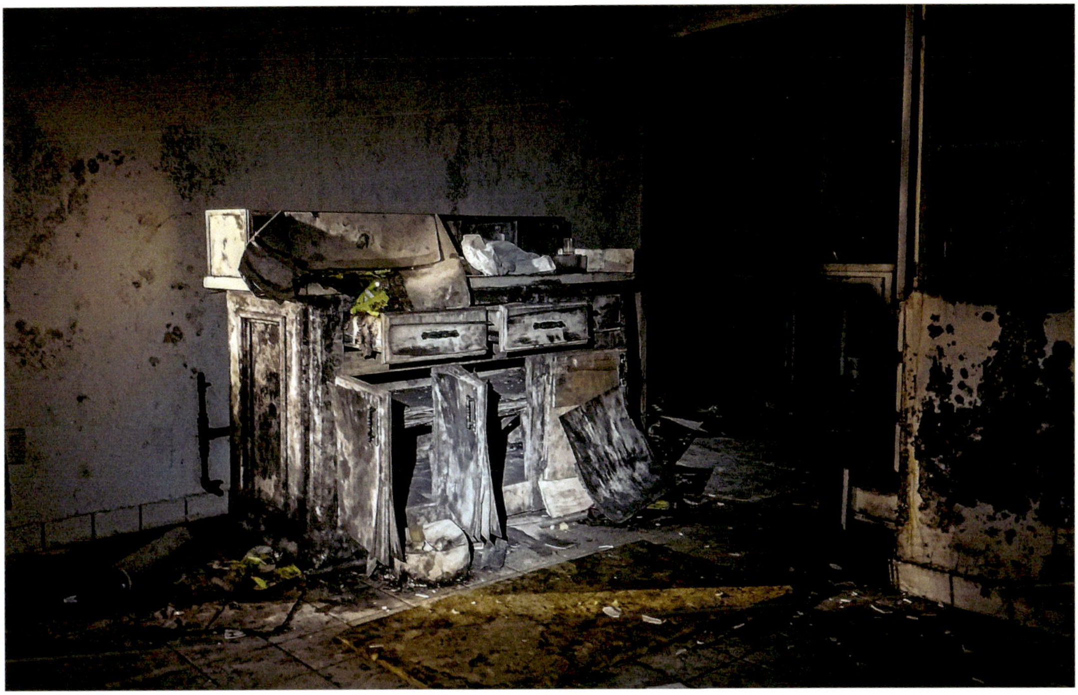

Extreme decay in the kitchen.

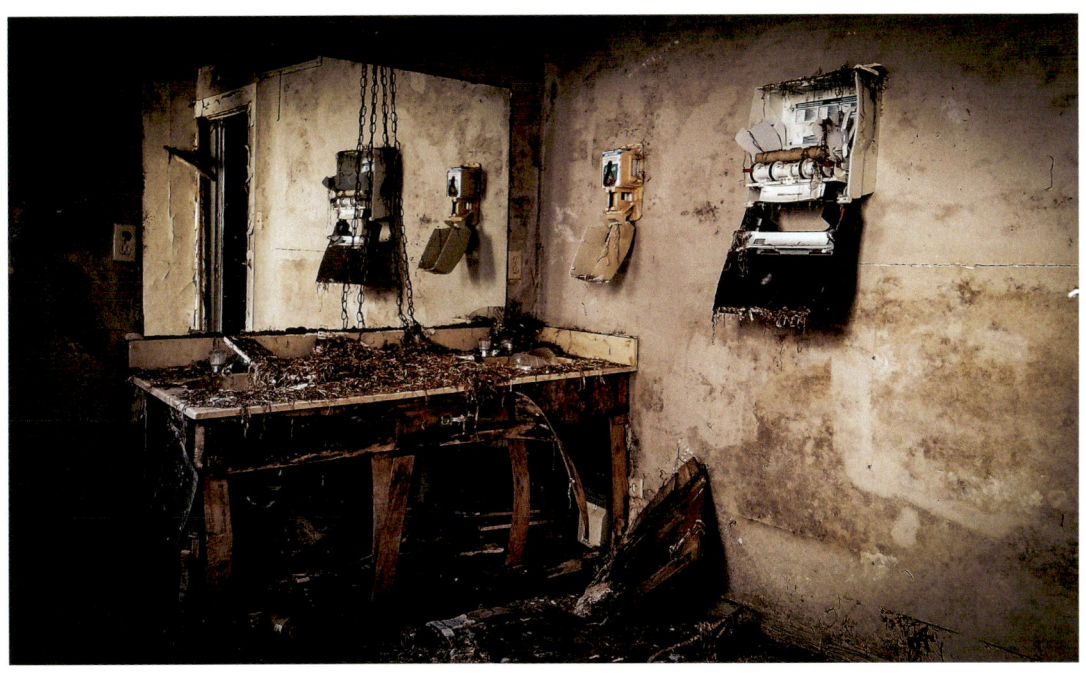

Decaying restroom with intact mirror.

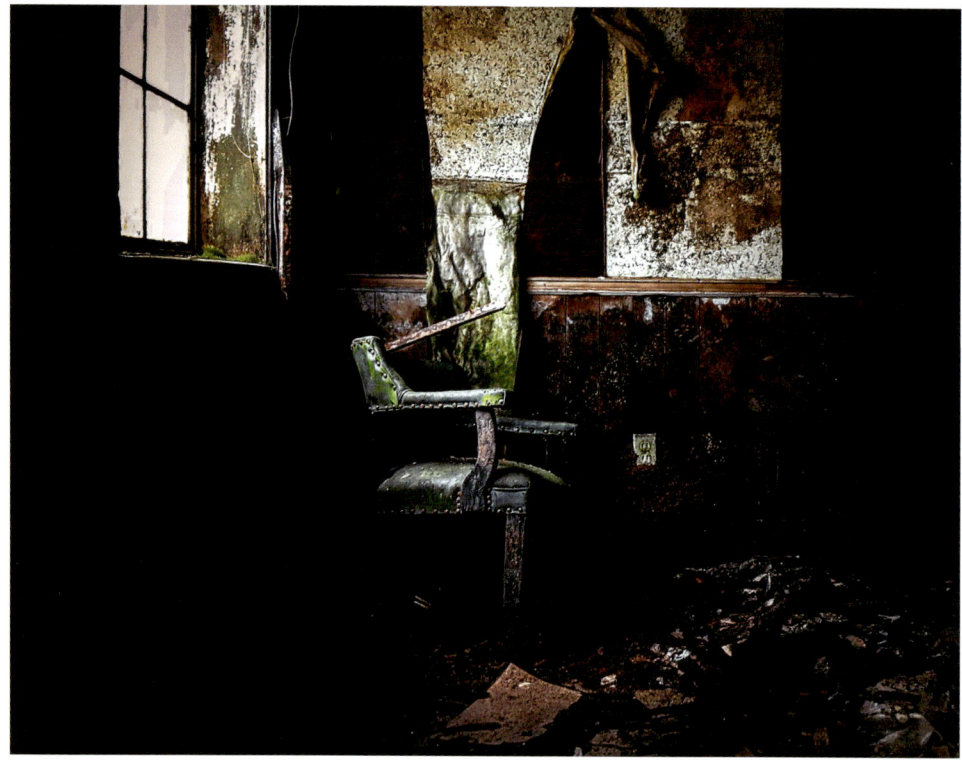

Abandoned, worn office chair.

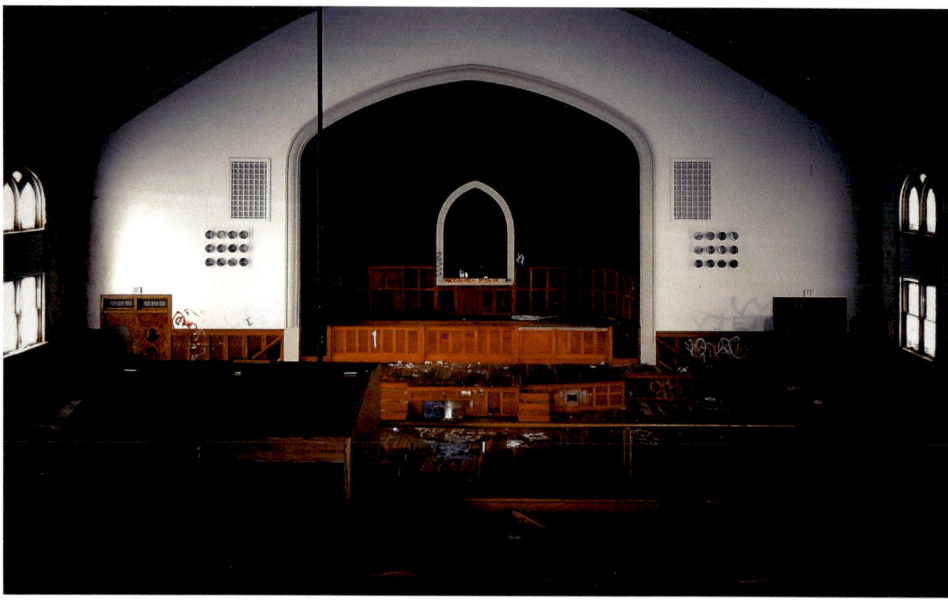

Main stage from upper seating.

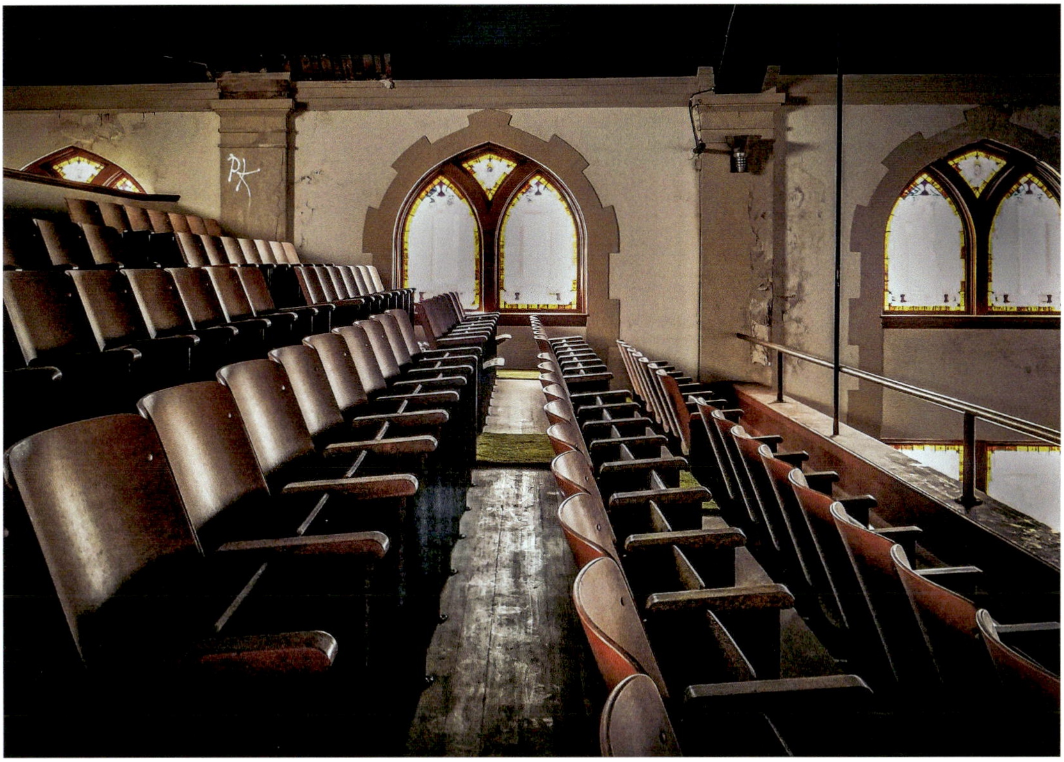

Upper deck view of the interior.

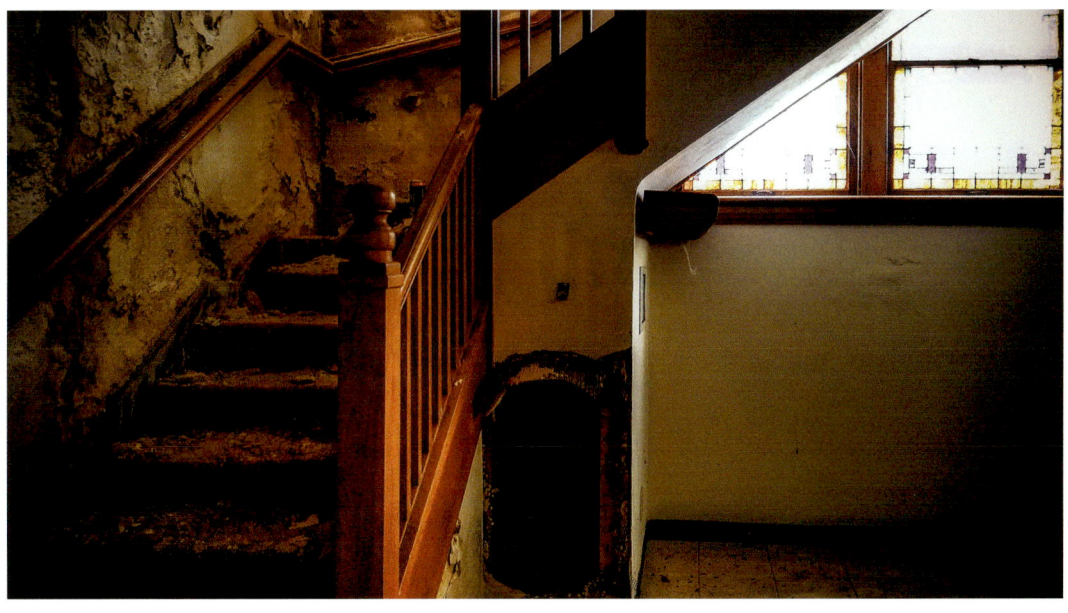

Staircase leading to administrative area.

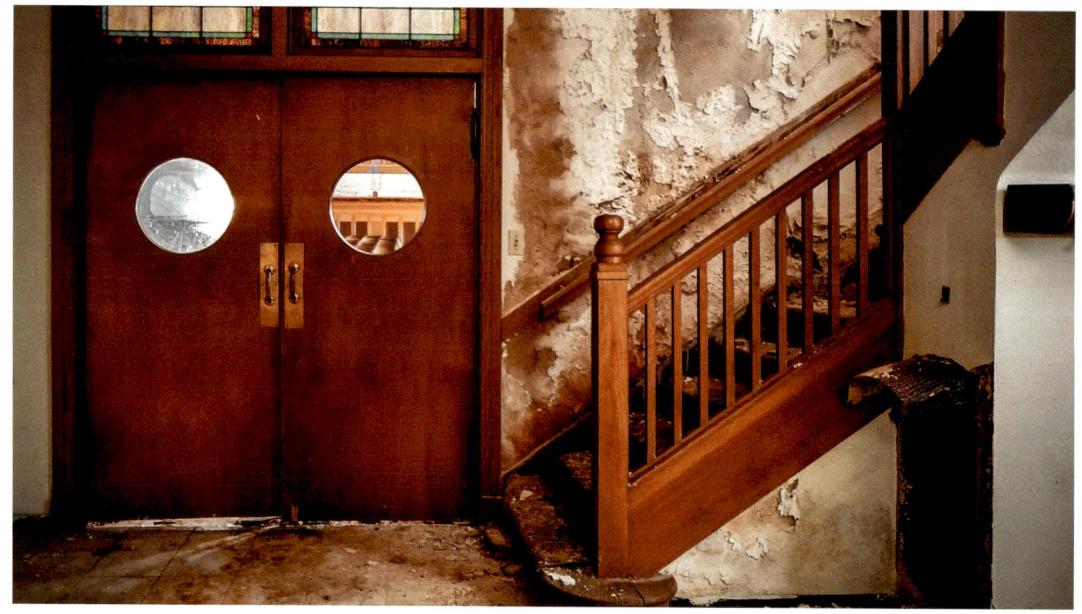

Worn staircase to administrative areas.

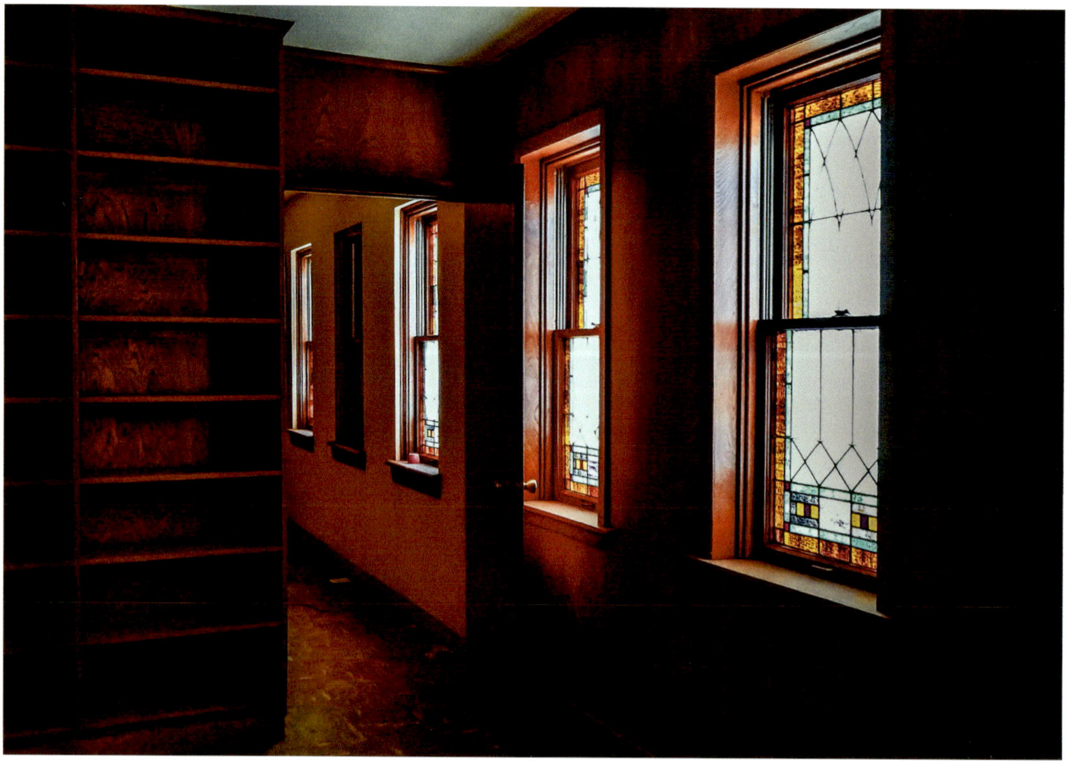

Bookcase and corridor in office area.

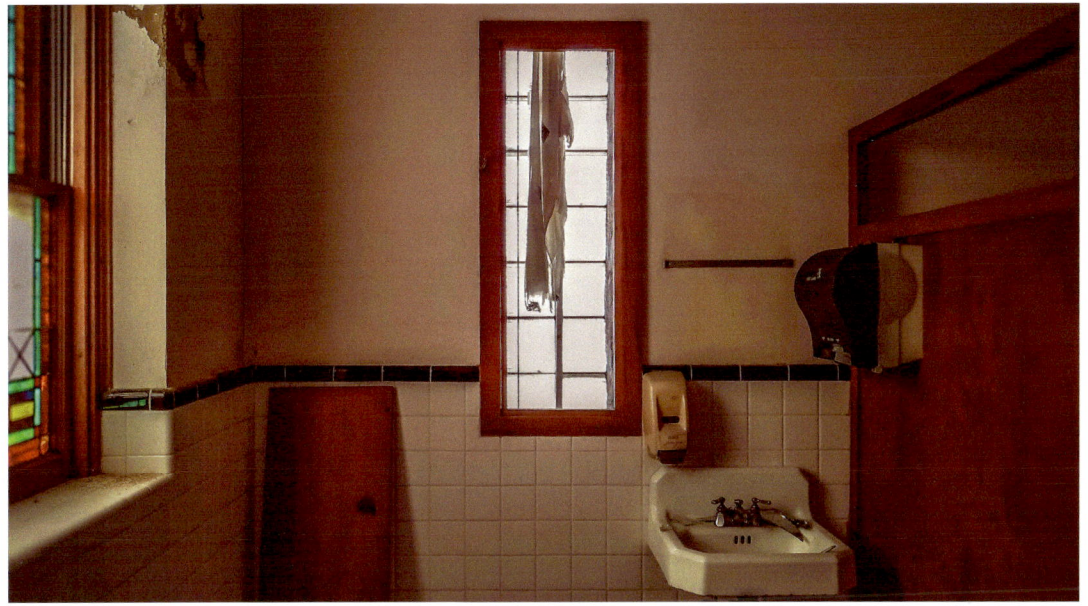

Restroom with stained glass intact.

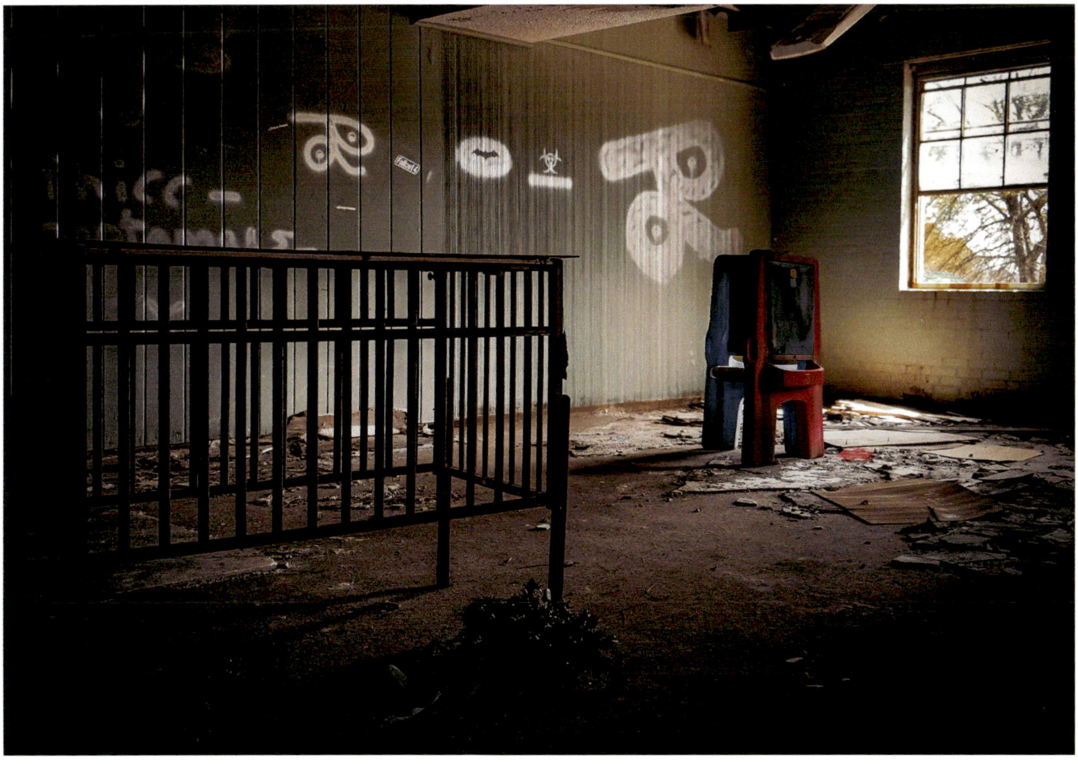

Derelict daycare within the church.

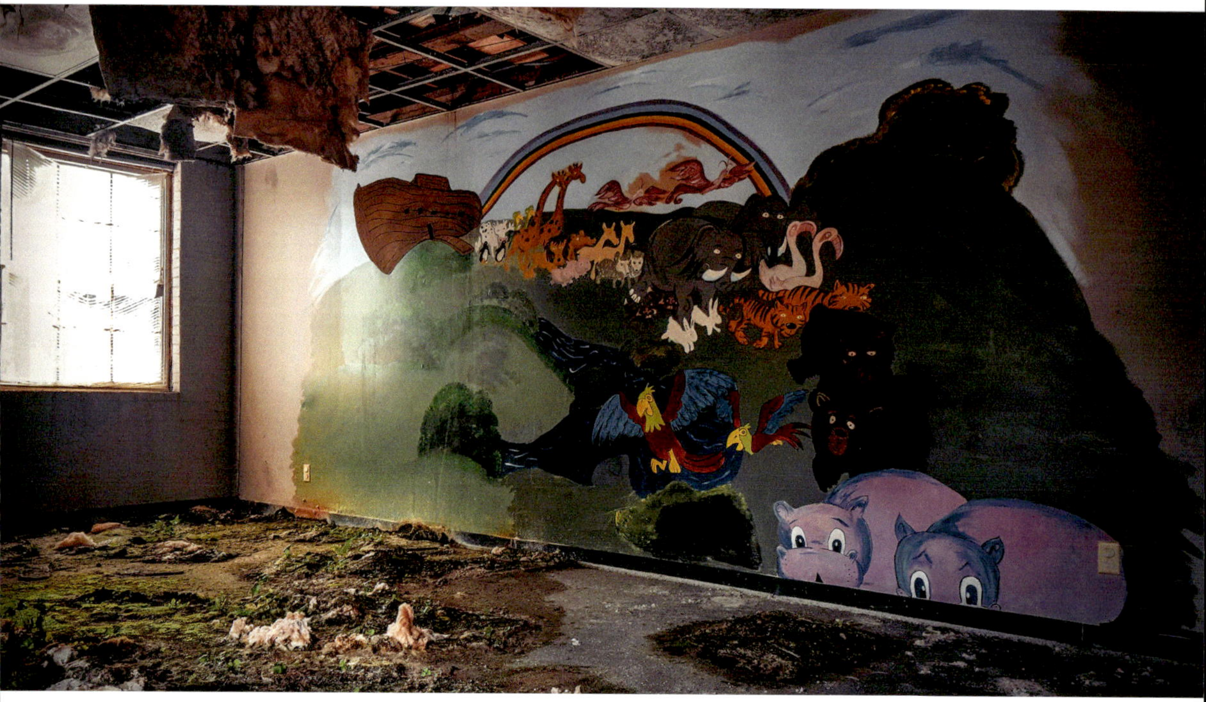

Faded mural in children's area.

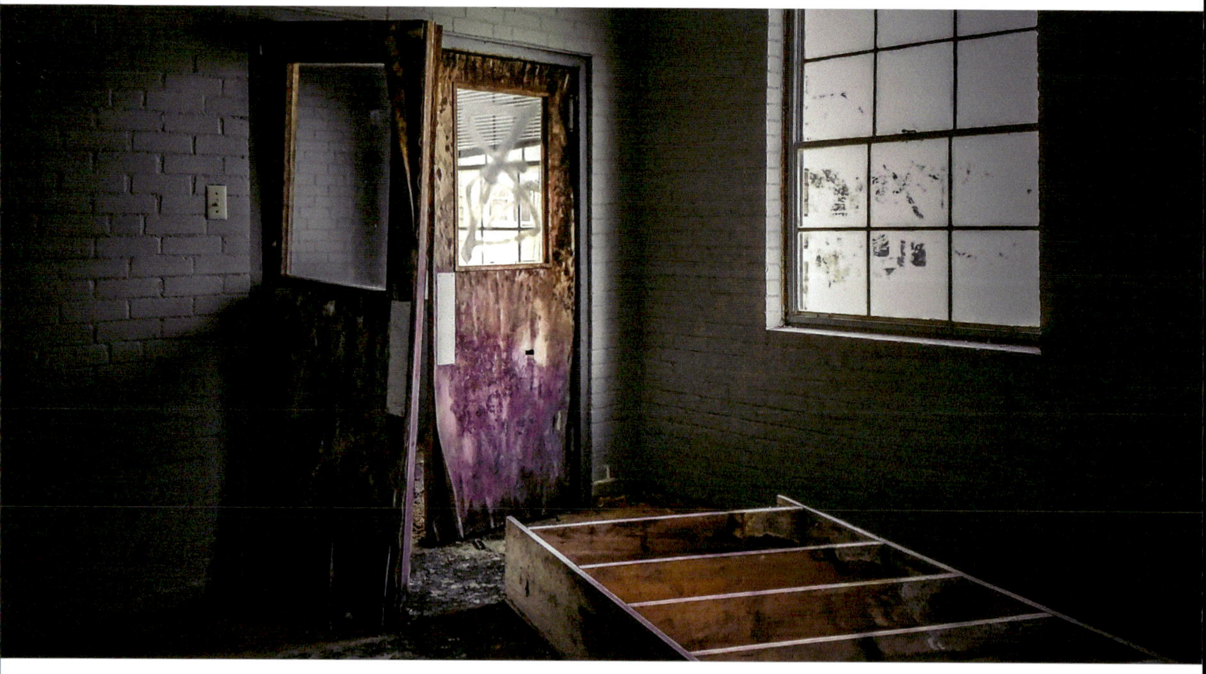

Decaying double doors.

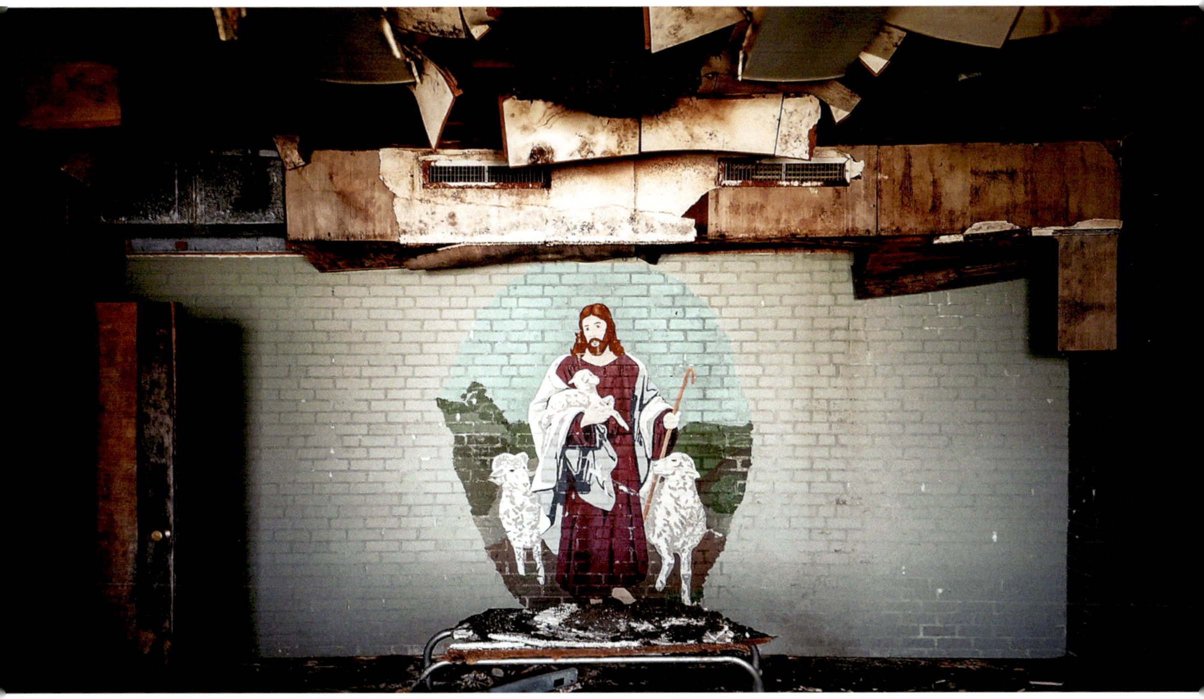

Mural of Christ and his flock.

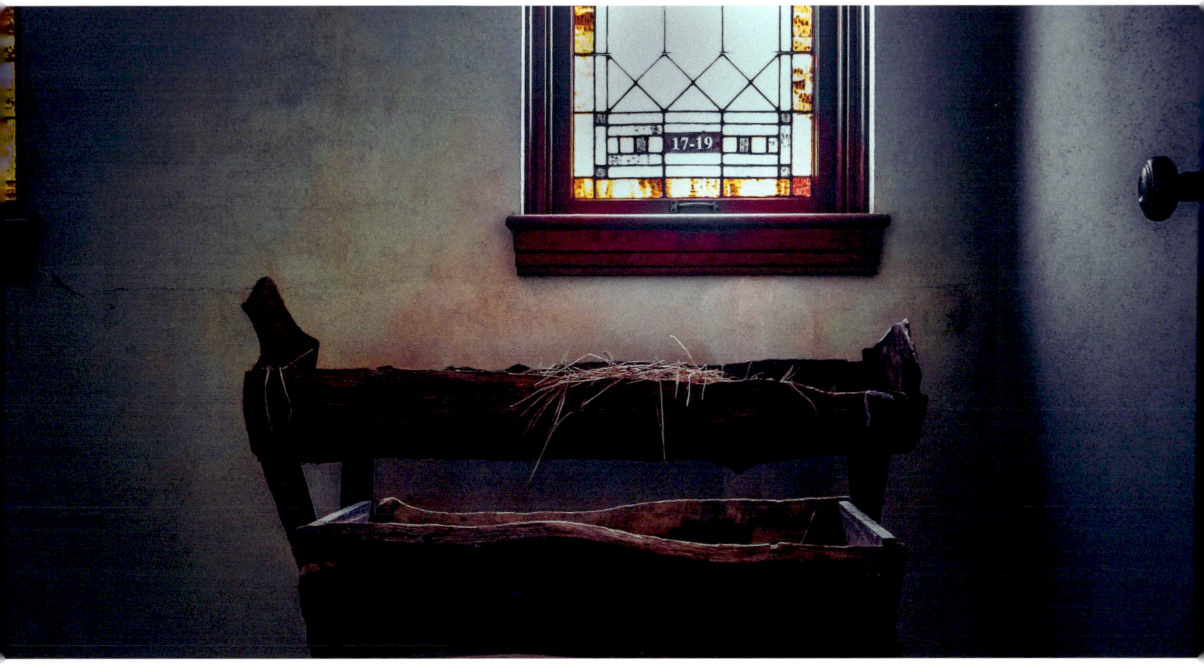

Dust-covered manger.

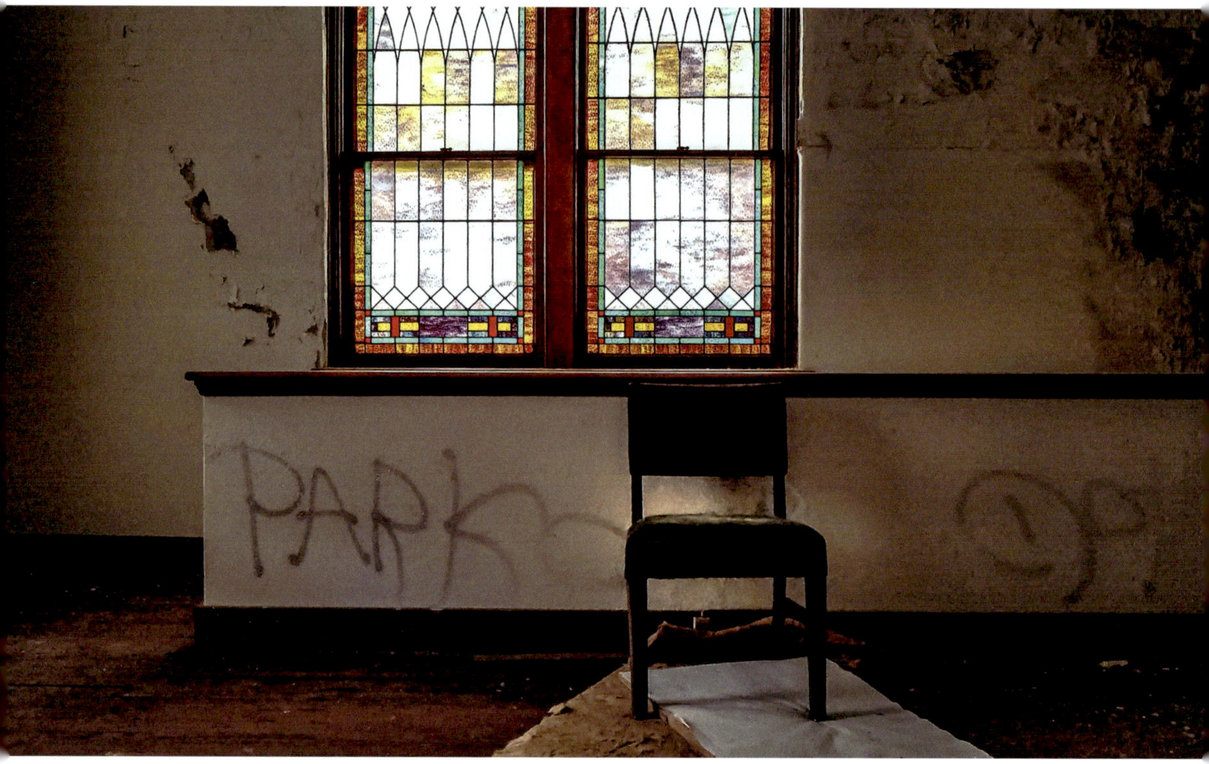

Graffiti, stained glass, and a lone chair.

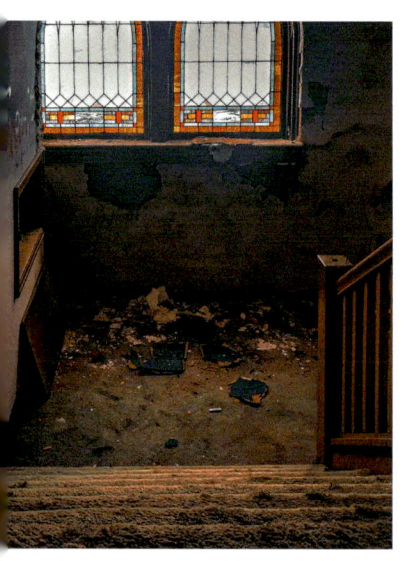

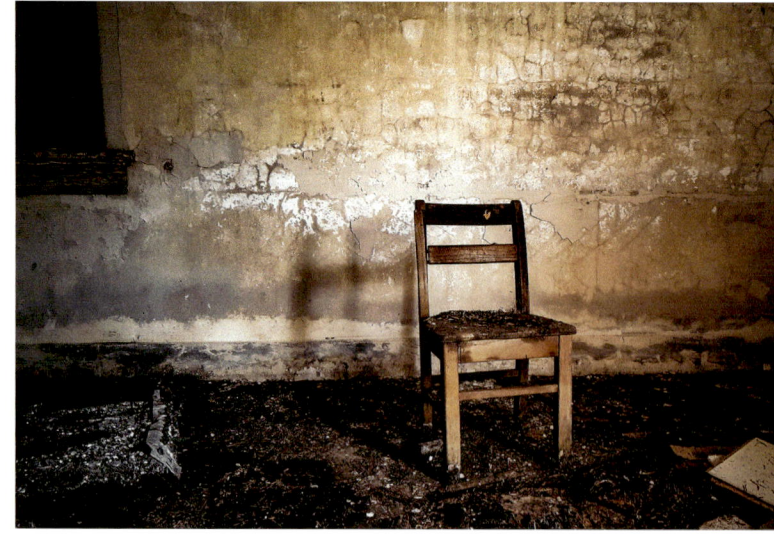

Above left: Faint light through stained glass.

Above right: Weathered chair left behind.

3

Doucette Union Church:
Tyler County, Doucette

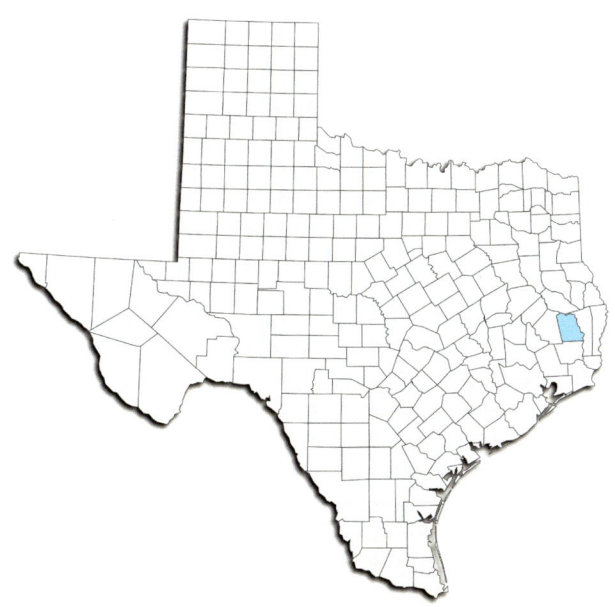

Created with paintmaps.com

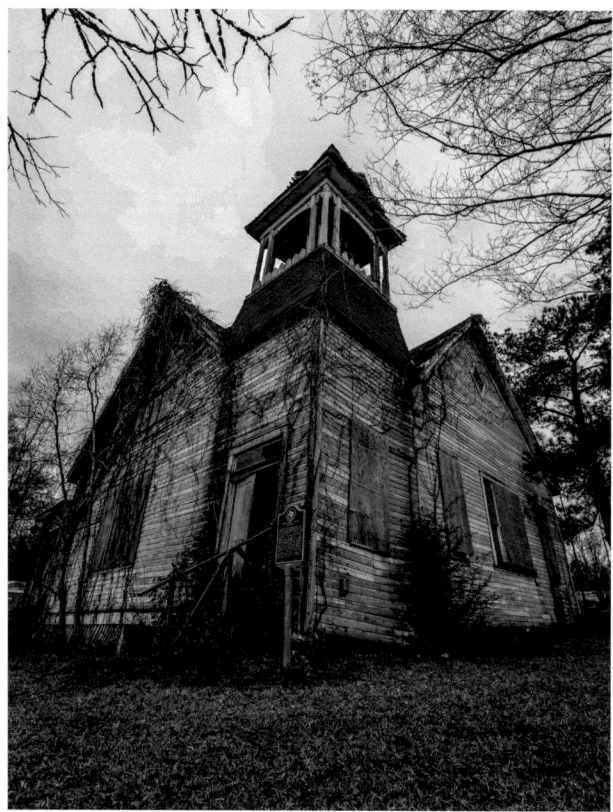

Low-angle shot highlighting architecture.

Doucette, Texas, emerged in the late nineteenth century as a bustling community tied to the timber industry. In the early 1890s, a sawmill was established by Hargiss, Doucette, and McCready, marking the beginning of a vibrant era for the town. Following Hargiss's departure, Fred and Pete Doucette, alongside William McCready, took the helm. The town's name was a tribute to the Doucette brothers, whose influence was instrumental in its growth.

Tragedy struck in 1896 when a catastrophic boiler explosion claimed the life of Fred Doucette and six other workers, shaking the tight-knit community to its core. Despite the loss, the mill persevered under Pete Doucette and McCready's leadership until it was sold to the Emporia Lumber Company around 1903. Over the years, the mill changed hands multiple times—from the Thompson Brothers to the Fidelity Lumber Company, and eventually to the Long-Bell Lumber Company, before being acquired by International Paper Company in 1956.

As a company town, Doucette revolved around the sawmill, with residents relying on it for jobs, housing, and essential services, creating both a sense of community and a precarious dependence on the mill's success.

Doucette's establishment of a post office in 1893, with William McCready as the first postmaster, marked another milestone in its development. The town quickly became a hub for both industry and community life. By 1908, the creation of the Doucette Union Church, which served Baptist, Methodist, and Presbyterian congregations, encouraged unity among

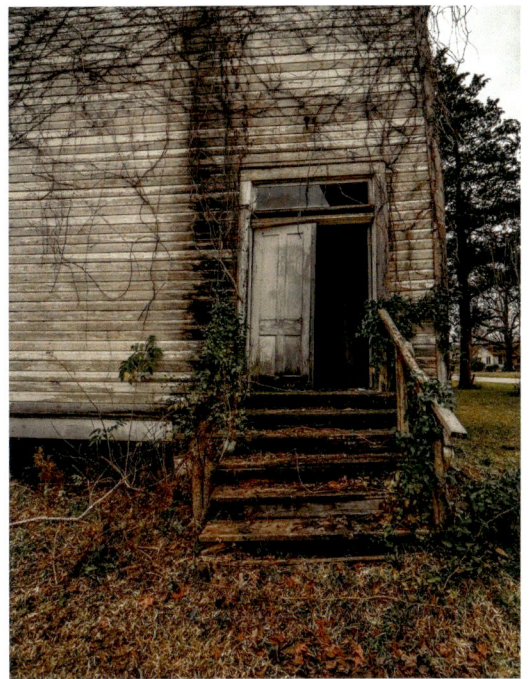
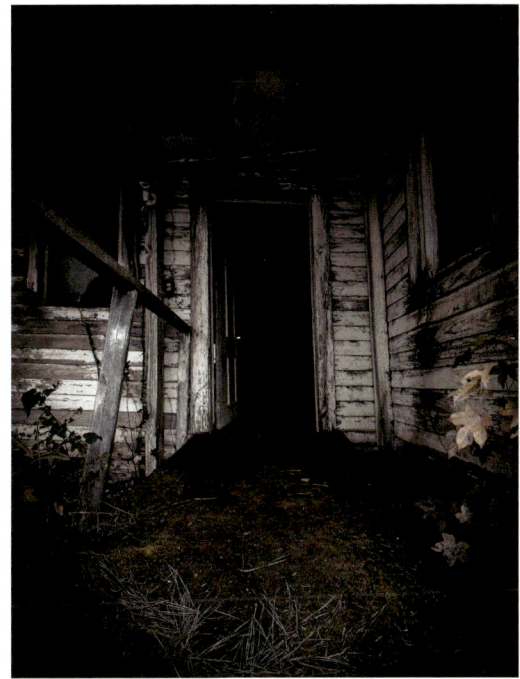

Above left: Close-up of main entrance.

Above right: Side entrance with accessibility ramp.

residents. For the residents of Doucette, life was often harsh and uncertain. The grueling demands of mill work, long hours, and the ever-present risks of injury created an atmosphere of physical and emotional strain. Families depended on the mill not only for their livelihoods but also for basic necessities, and any disruption in operations could mean economic ruin.

In this tough environment, the Doucette Union Church served as a sanctuary—a place to lay down burdens, seek solace, and find hope. Beyond spiritual guidance, the church offered a sense of stability and connection. The rotating ministers from different denominations symbolized unity in diversity, and amid the struggles of daily life, the church became a beacon of resilience. It was where neighbors supported one another through times of grief, celebrated moments of joy, and sought the strength to endure.

However, as the twentieth century progressed, the lumber industry began to wane. Resource depletion and evolving economic conditions led to job losses and a shrinking population. Many residents left in search of better opportunities, leaving behind a quieter Doucette.

Today, the town stands as a testament to its rich history and the resilience of its people. Efforts by the Tyler County Historical Commission to preserve the Doucette Union Church highlight the enduring importance of the town's legacy. Though its bustling days are long gone, Doucette remains a place of historical pride, offering a glimpse into the community that once thrived amidst the towering pines of East Texas.

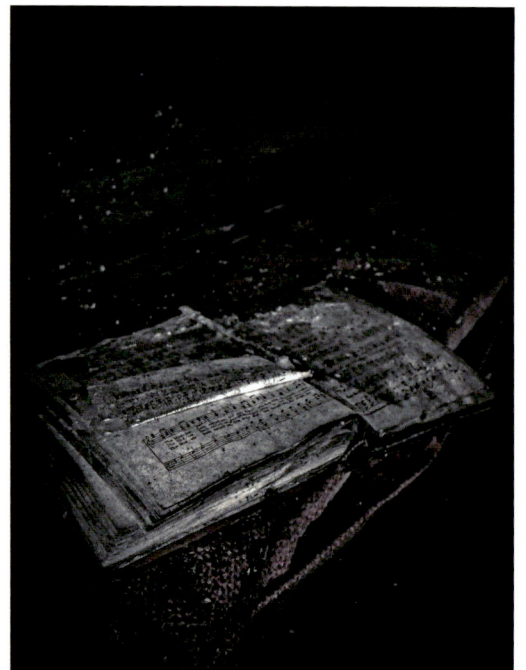

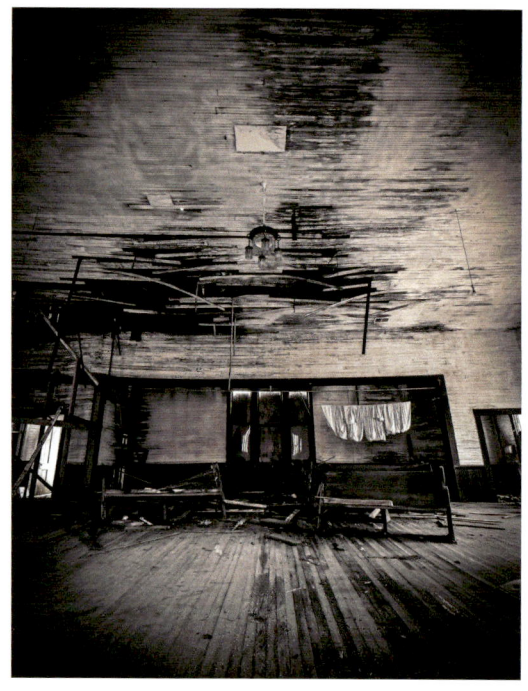

Above left: Decaying hymnal left behind.

Above right: Stage view of empty congregation.

Left: Main stage stripped of grandeur.

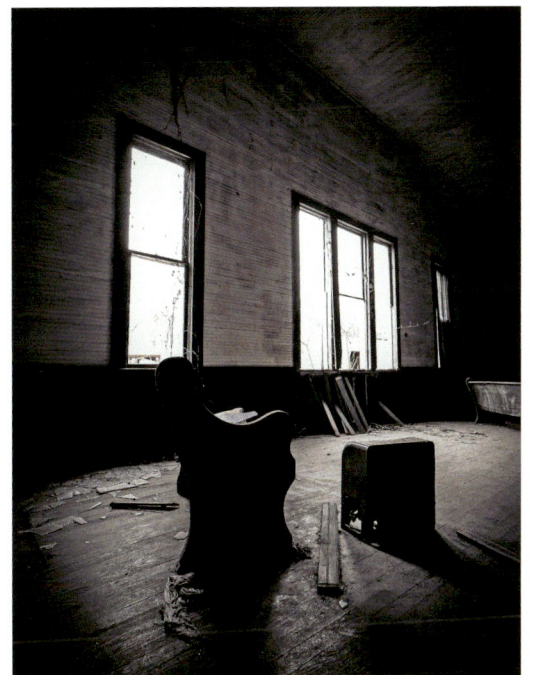

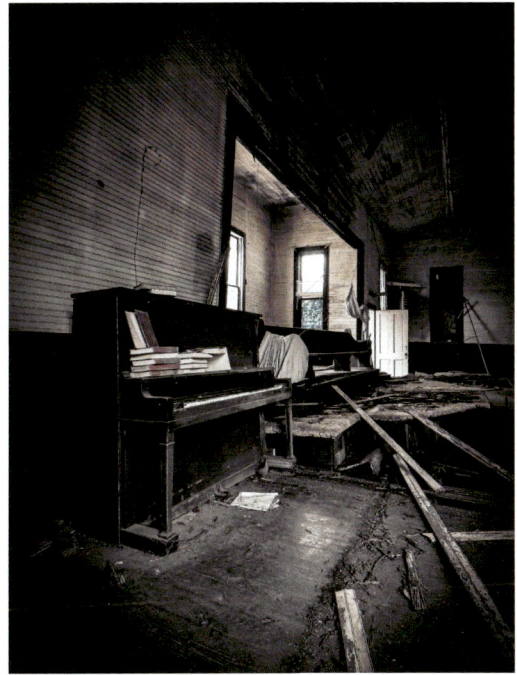

Above left: Artistic view of an old pew.

Above right: Silent piano next to stage.

Right: Foyer view toward entrance.

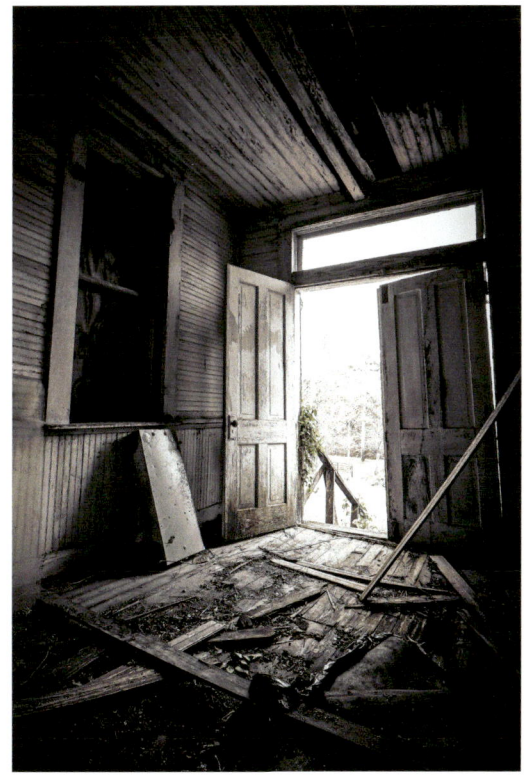

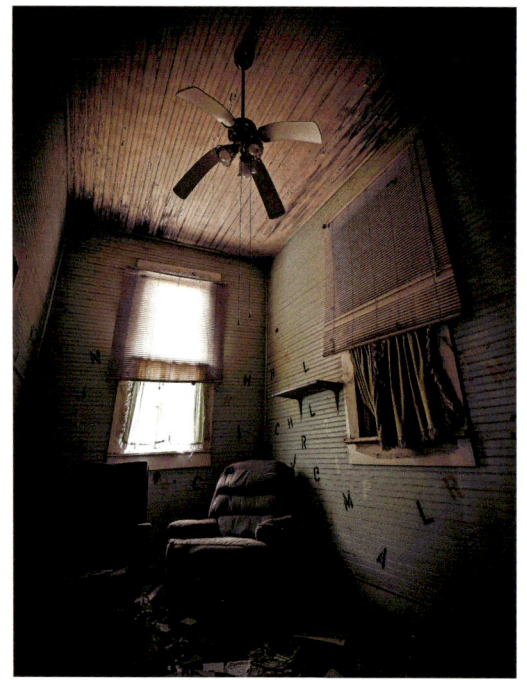

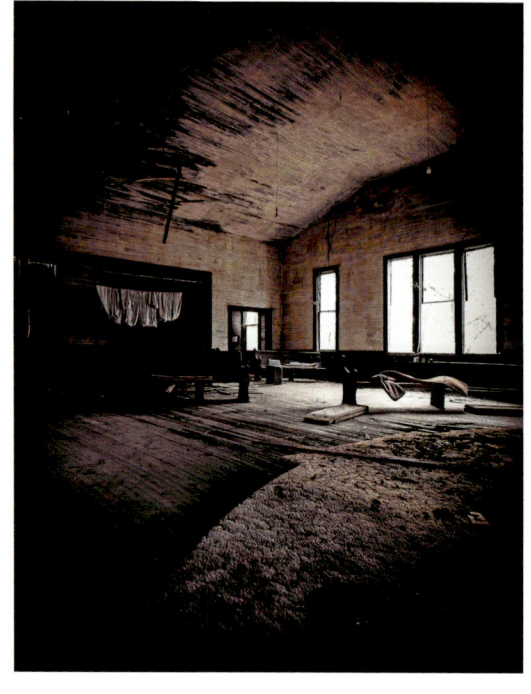

Above left: Tiny children's room still intact.

Above right: Left corner view of encroaching decay.

Left: Hymnal on a broken pew.

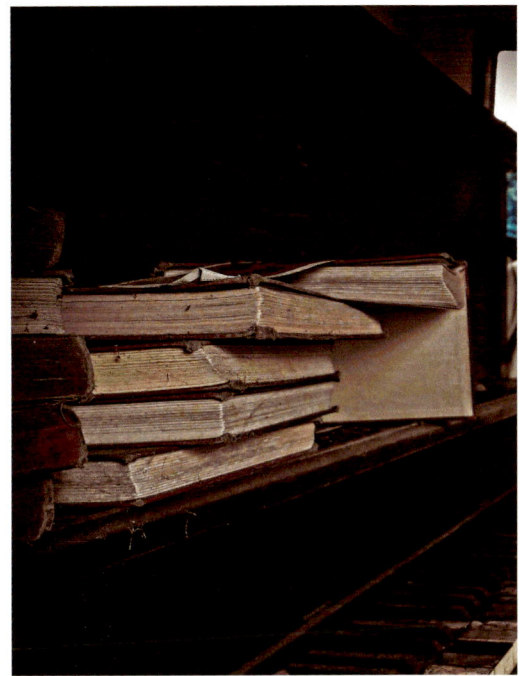

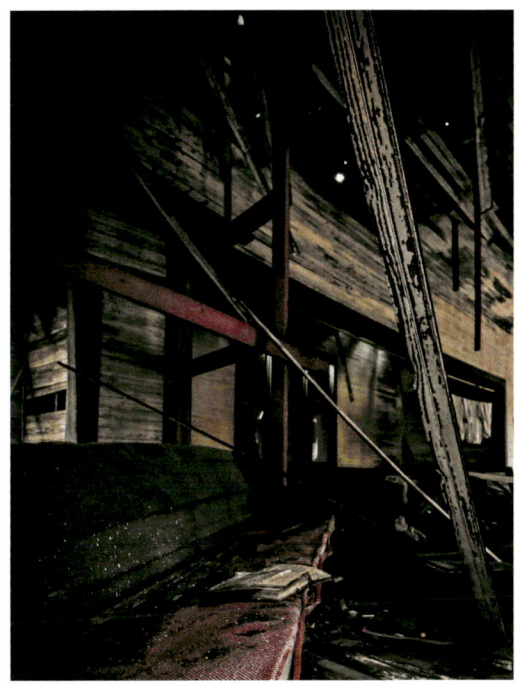

Above left: Forgotten hymnals.

Above right: Ceiling caving under decay.

Right: Exterior with enduring bell tower.

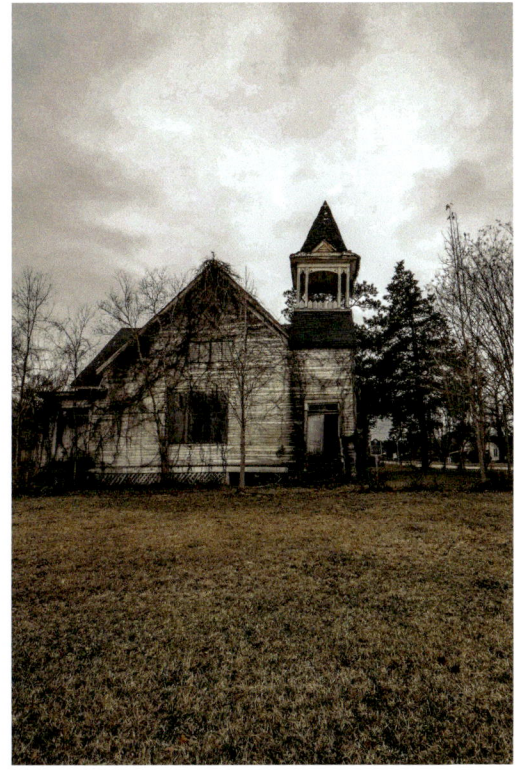

4

St. Joseph Church: Milam County, Rockdale

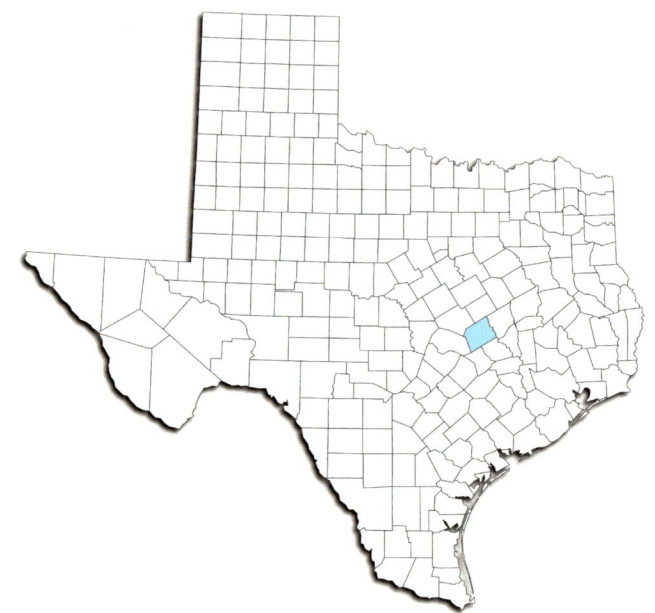

Created with paintmaps.com

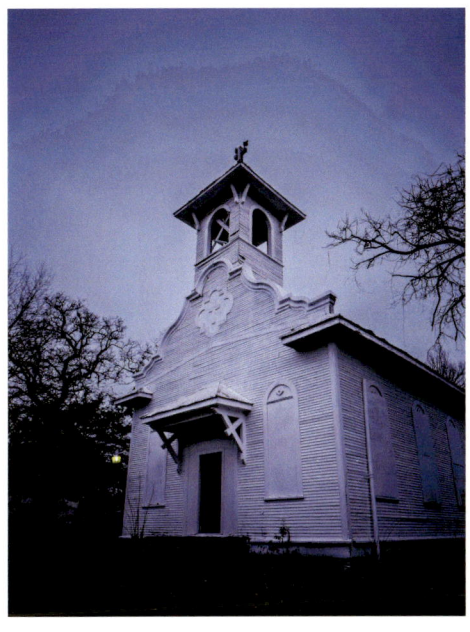

Ornate awning and bell tower details.

Milam County, Texas, has always been a place shaped by movement—people moving in search of opportunity, industries rising and falling, and towns fluctuating between prosperity and decline. Rockdale was once at the center of it all, established in the 1870s as the railroad expanded across Texas. What began as a small agricultural settlement transformed into a thriving industrial town.

The arrival of the Aluminum Company of America (ALCOA) in the 1950s changed everything. The plant, known as the Rockdale Works, was built to refine bauxite-the ore from which aluminum is extracted-using power generated by the nearby Sandow Power Plant. The facility operated as a fully integrated production site, meaning it handled every step of the aluminum-making process, from mining and refining to casting and fabrication. Bauxite was extracted from deposits in Milam County and transported to the plant, where it underwent the Hall-Héroult process, a method that required an immense amount of electricity to separate pure aluminum from alumina. To sustain the high energy demands of this process, the Sandow Power Plant was constructed specifically for ALCOA's operations, ensuring a steady power supply that kept the plant running efficiently. Once refined, the aluminum was cast into ingots, sheets, and other industrial forms, supplying materials for automobile production, aerospace manufacturing, and construction industries.

At its peak, ALCOA employed over 2,000 workers, and the company's presence reshaped Rockdale in ways few could have anticipated. The plant did more than provide jobs—it transformed the town itself. Families moved in, schools expanded, and small businesses flourished to support the growing workforce. ALCOA invested in local infrastructure, building roads and housing, making Rockdale one of the most economically stable communities in Milam County. For decades, the town thrived under the plant's success, with its residents confident that Rockdale's prosperity would continue.

But the success didn't last forever. By the early 2000s, market shifts, rising energy costs, and growing international competition placed financial strain on ALCOA's operations. The aluminum industry was changing, and Rockdale's once-thriving plant was no longer as competitive as it had been in previous decades. In 2008, the Rockdale Works plant was permanently shut down, marking the end of an era. The closure devastated the local economy, leaving thousands without jobs and forcing many families to leave in search of work elsewhere. Businesses that had once relied on the steady flow of ALCOA workers struggled to stay open, and Rockdale's population began to dwindle. What had once been an industrial powerhouse became a town grappling with economic uncertainty, its streets quieter and its future uncertain.

Yet, through all these changes, St. Joseph Catholic Church endured. Established in 1874 by European immigrants, the church had been a constant presence in Rockdale through every boom and bust.

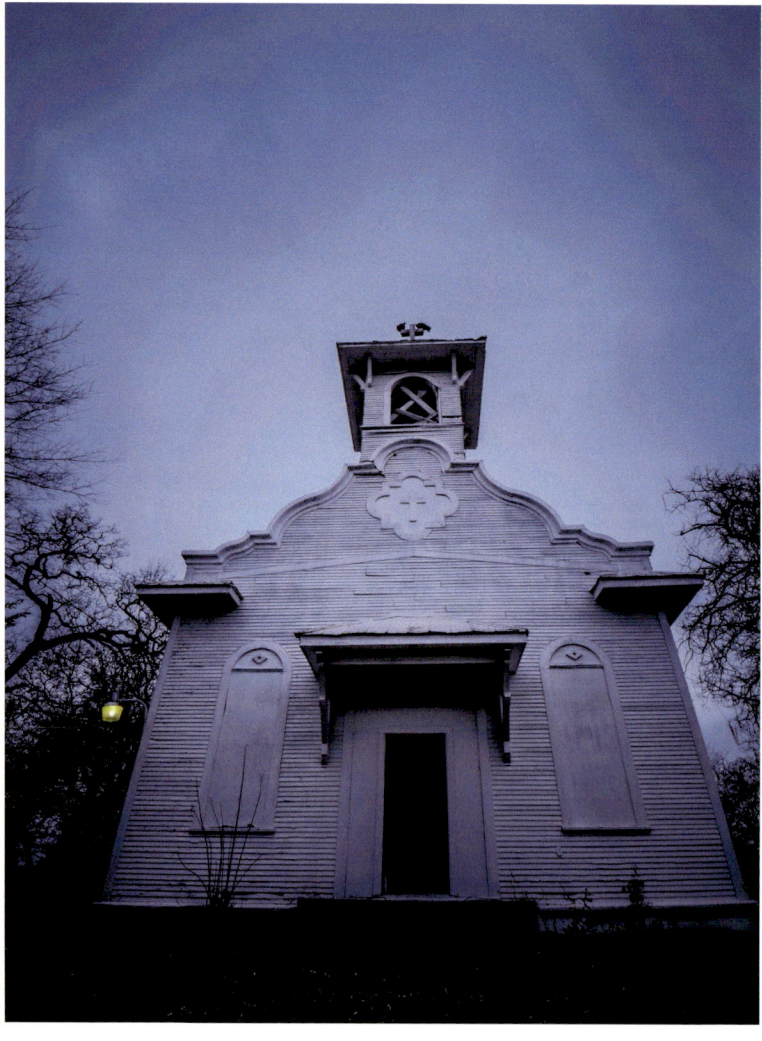

St. Joseph Church exterior.

By 1890, St. Joseph had become a mission of the nearby town of Cameron, meaning it was administered and supported by the local parish there. While this allowed the church to continue its services, it also meant that priest visits were infrequent, and resources were often stretched thin. Despite these challenges, St. Joseph remained a central gathering place for the Catholic community. A small Catholic school was later established, providing education rooted in faith, though it eventually closed due to financial constraints and changing demographics.

In 1912, as the congregation grew, the church dedicated a new building, replacing the original structure with a larger, more permanent place of worship. During this period, Rockdale continued to expand, fueled by agriculture, coal mining, and the promise of industrial development. The church played an essential role in supporting families through both prosperity and hardship.

As Rockdale's demographics evolved, so did St. Joseph. Spanish Masses were originally held at nearby St. Anne Church until 1924, when its parishioners merged with St. Joseph, further enriching the diversity of the congregation. However, the economic hardships of the 1930s and 1940s brought new challenges, including a decline in both population and parishioners. Yet, with the support of devoted members and benefactors like H. H. Coffield, St. Joseph persevered.

It survived the Great Depression, adapted to changing demographics, and weathered the collapse of the industries that once sustained the town. Even as families moved away, St. Joseph remained, a testament to the resilience of the community and the faith that bound it together.

By 1967, Rockdale was experiencing one of its most significant periods of growth due to the rise of ALCOA. To accommodate this expansion, St. Joseph constructed a third church building. The church continued to evolve, adding educational facilities and constructing a new academic building in 1985 to further serve its parishioners.

The closure of the ALCOA plant in 2008 was a devastating blow to Rockdale, leading to job losses, and a gradual population decline. Yet, through this period of hardship, St. Joseph remained steadfast. In 2014, the third church underwent extensive renovations, funded by the Will S. and Mildred K. Palmer Memorial Fund, ensuring that it would continue to serve the community for generations to come.

While the second church building remains unused, St. Joseph's legacy endures. More than just a place of worship, it has been a witness to Rockdale's transformations—standing through the town's early agricultural roots, its industrial rise, and its struggles with economic downturns. As Rockdale continues to redefine itself, St. Joseph remains a symbol of faith, resilience, and the unwavering spirit of the people who have called this community home.

Today, Rockdale is still searching for a way forward, though there are efforts to repurpose the former ALCOA site into a power-generation facility, bringing hope that industry might return in a new form. Rockdale's history is one of adaptation, shaped by the forces of industry and faith, with St. Joseph Church standing as a reminder that some foundations remain strong no matter how much the world around them changes. It's a story not unlike those of Clarkson and Sharp, where faith outlived prosperity, and churches became the lasting landmarks of communities that transformed with time.

5

Clarkson Baptist Church: Milam County, Clarkson

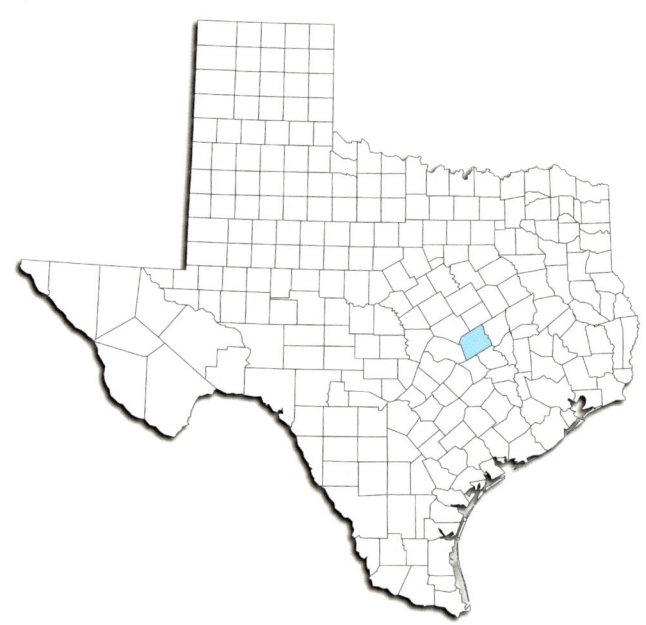

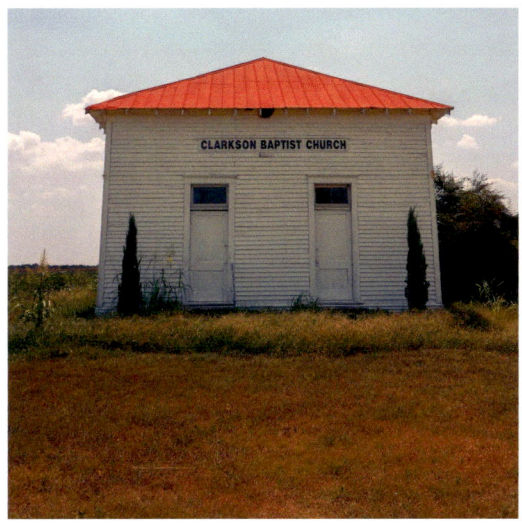

Modest exterior with hidden beauty.

Clarkson, just 28 miles north of Rockdale, shares a similar story—one of hope, growth, and decline. Founded in the late nineteenth century, the town initially flourished thanks to agriculture, drawing families to the fertile land along the Brazos River. Cotton was king, and farming sustained Clarkson for decades.

By the early 1900s, Clarkson had built the foundations of a thriving community, including schools in line with the segregated education system of the time. In 1903, the town had a one-teacher school for forty-three White students and a two-teacher school for 105 Black students. These schools were small, but they represented a commitment to education in a rural town where opportunities were often limited. However, as the population declined, so did the need for local schools. By the early 1950s, Clarkson's schools were consolidated into the Cameron Independent School District, signaling the town's decreasing ability to sustain its own institutions.

At the same time, Clarkson Baptist Church was the heart of the town, a place where farmers met after long days in the fields and children grew up learning the traditions of their families. Even as the schoolhouses emptied and young residents moved away in search of better opportunities, the church stood as a constant presence.

But as the decades passed, farming practices changed. Mechanization reduced the need for labor, and younger generations left for opportunities elsewhere. By 2000, only ten residents remained in what was once a hopeful settlement. The closure of ALCOA in Rockdale only further eroded the surrounding towns, taking away the last remaining economic support.

And yet, the church still stands, its wooden walls weathered by the passing time. Inside, the air is thick with history—dust settling on pews where families once gathered, and fading echoes of voices that have long since gone.

Clarkson's story, much like Rockdale's, is one of resilience. And just a few miles away, in Sharp, another church tells a similar tale of perseverance in a county where faith outlasted industry.

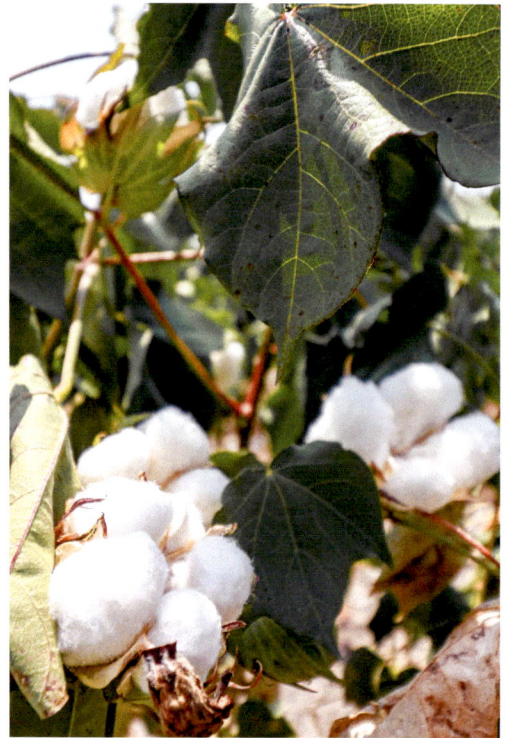

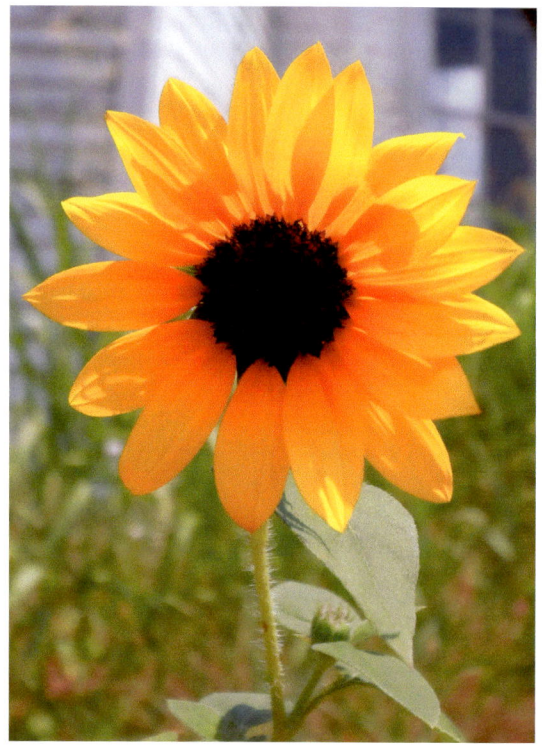

Above left: Cotton growing nearby.

Above right: Sunflower outside the church.

Left: Overgrown grass
surrounding the grounds.

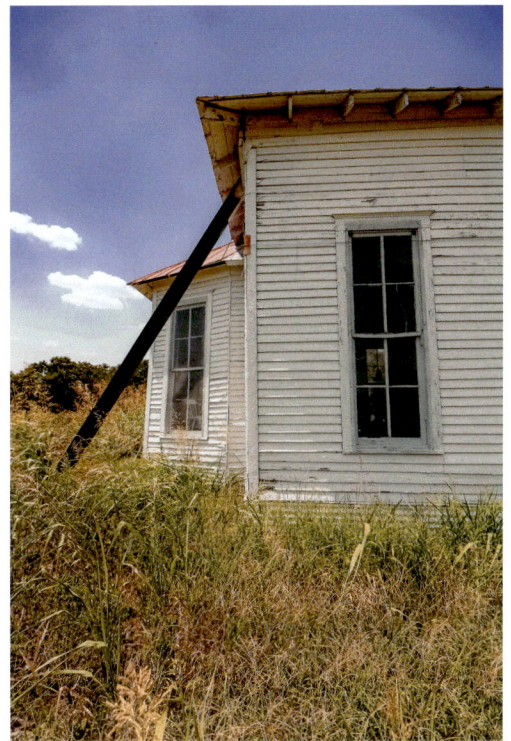

Exterior view of the church's rear.

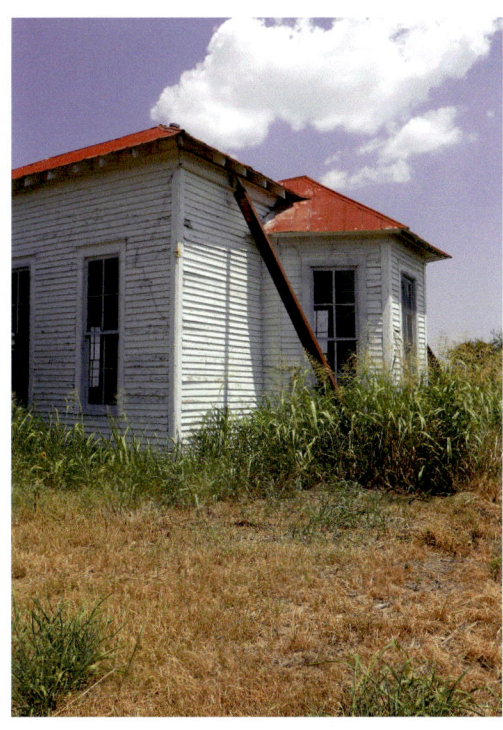

View of the back near the stage

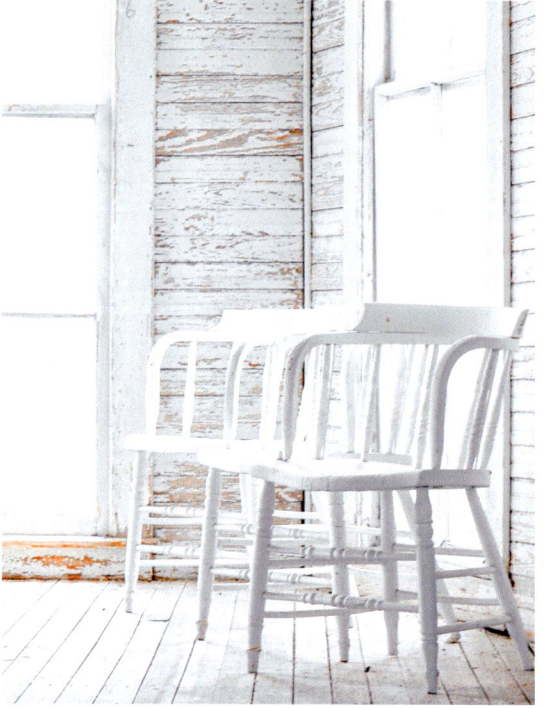

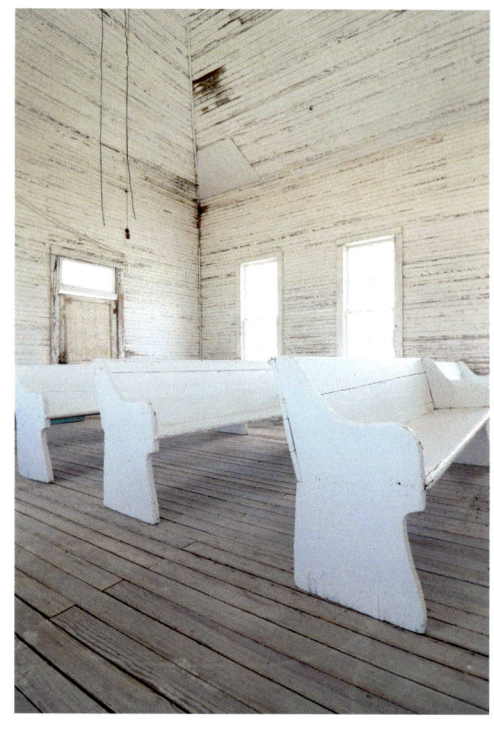

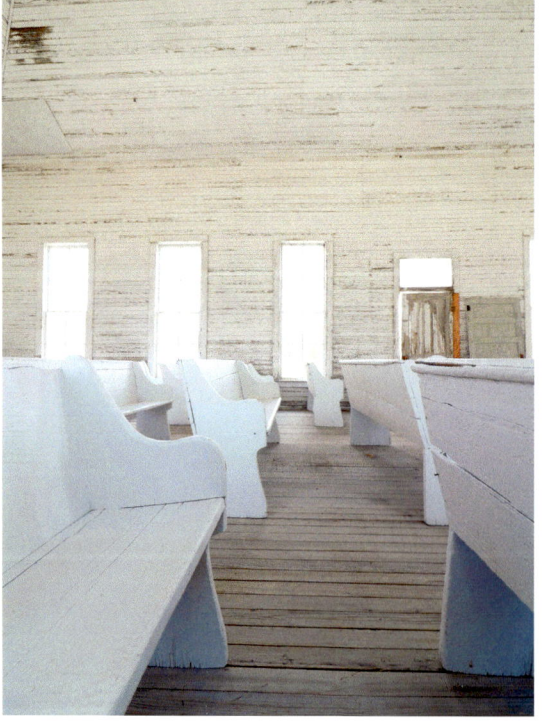

Above left: White chairs
on the main stage.

Above right: Quiet, empty white pews.

Left: Daylight filtering through windows.

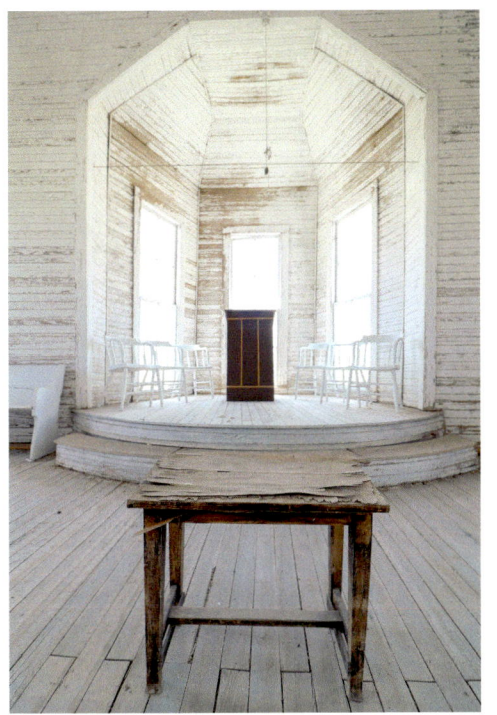

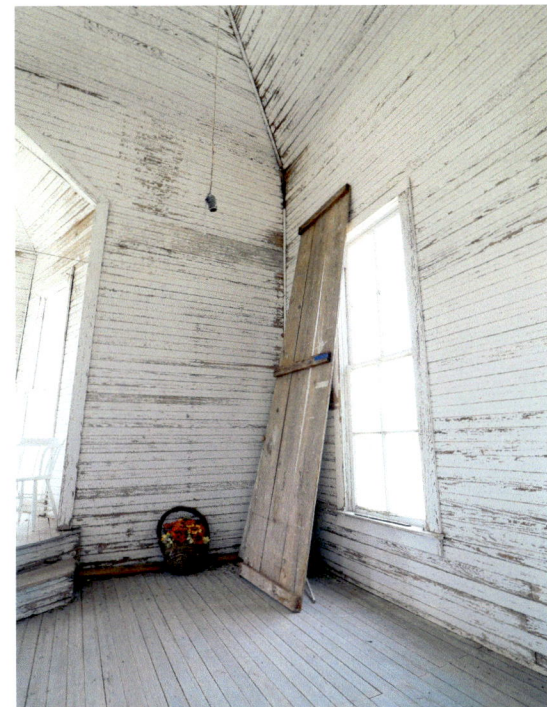

Above left: The main stage.

Above right: Items left behind in the church.

Right: Humble main entrance.

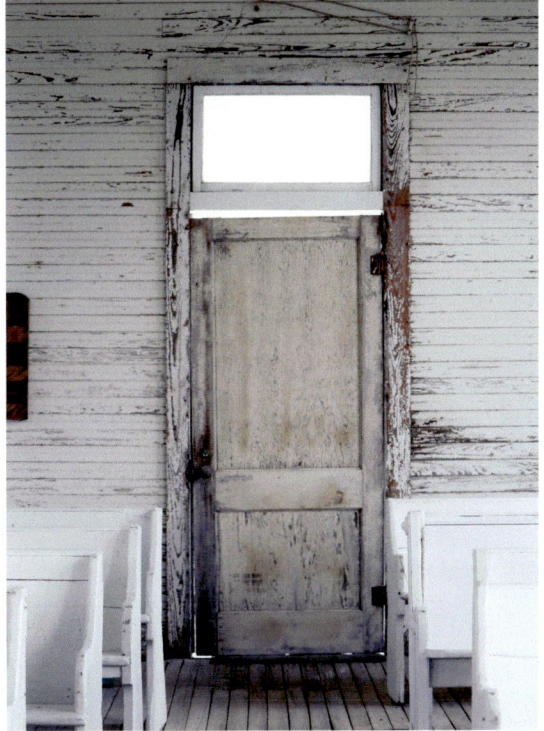

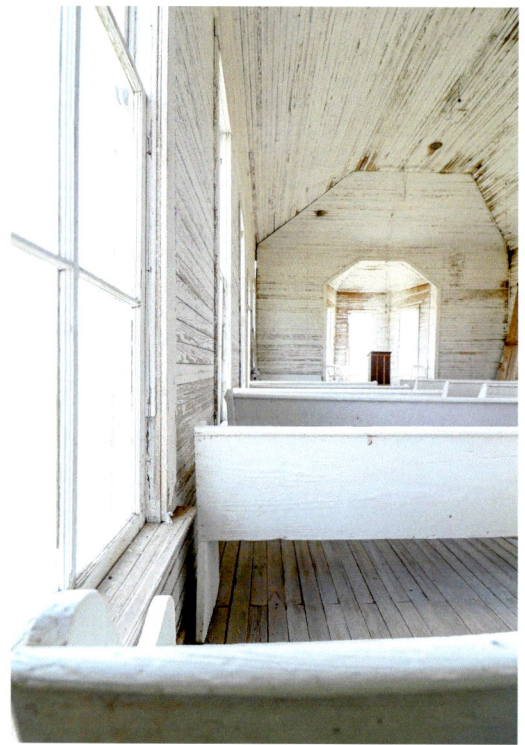

Rear pew view toward the stage.

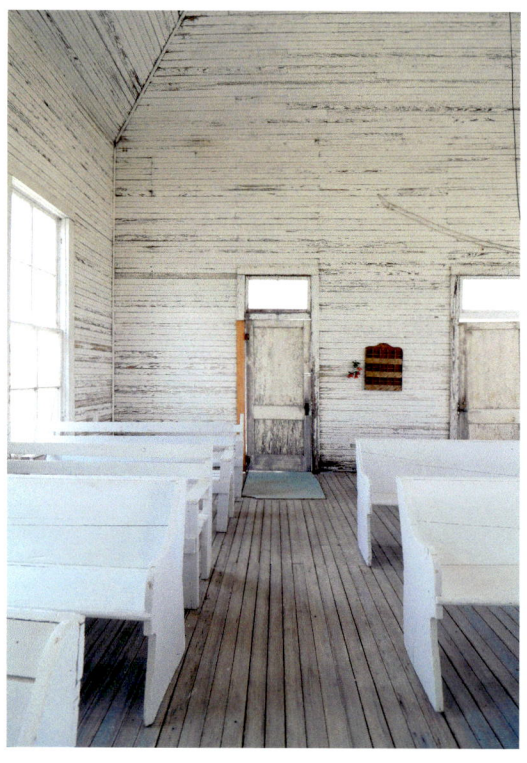

Empty central aisle.

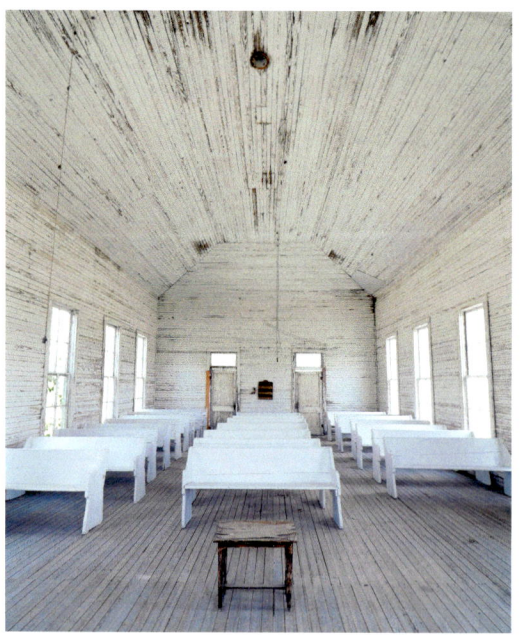

Stage view with hexagonal ceiling.

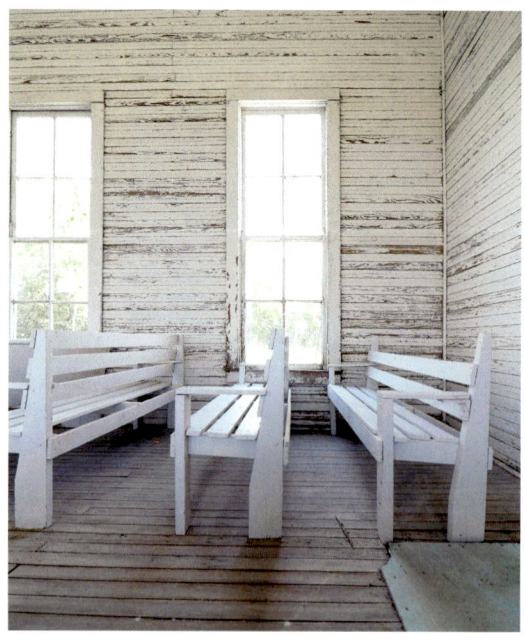

Neatly arranged pews.

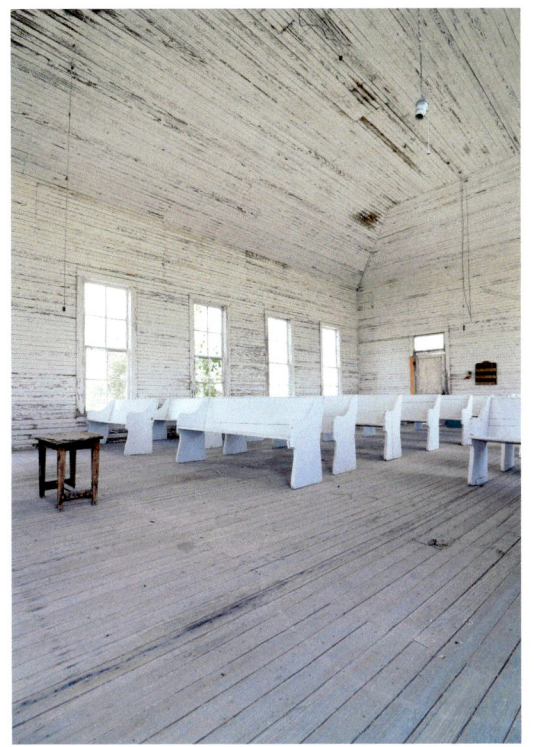

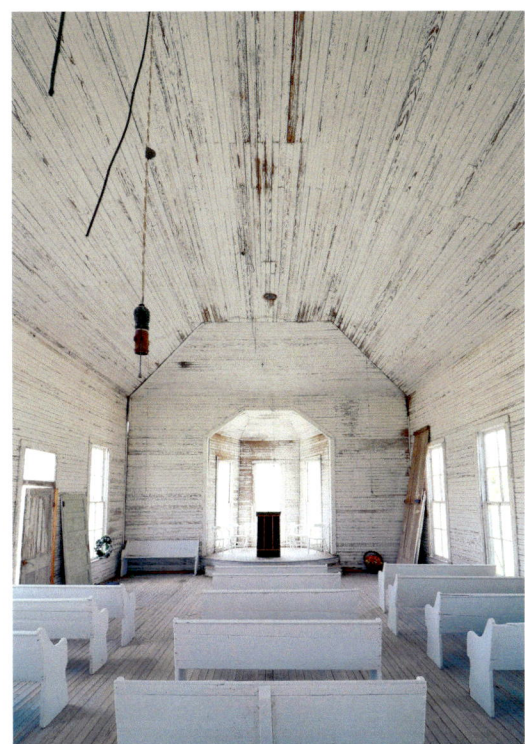

Above left: I spent time rearranging and cleaning the pews under mid-summer Texas heat.

Above right: Rear view toward the main stage.

Right: Wide shot toward the front entrance.

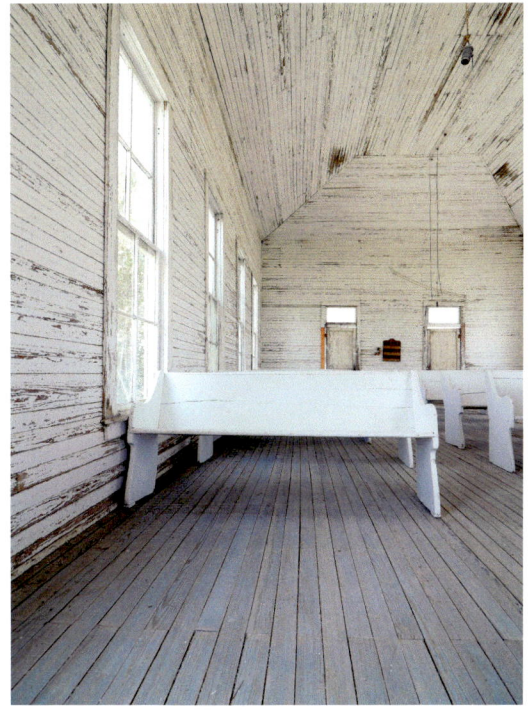

6

Sharp Presbyterian Church: Milam County, Sharp

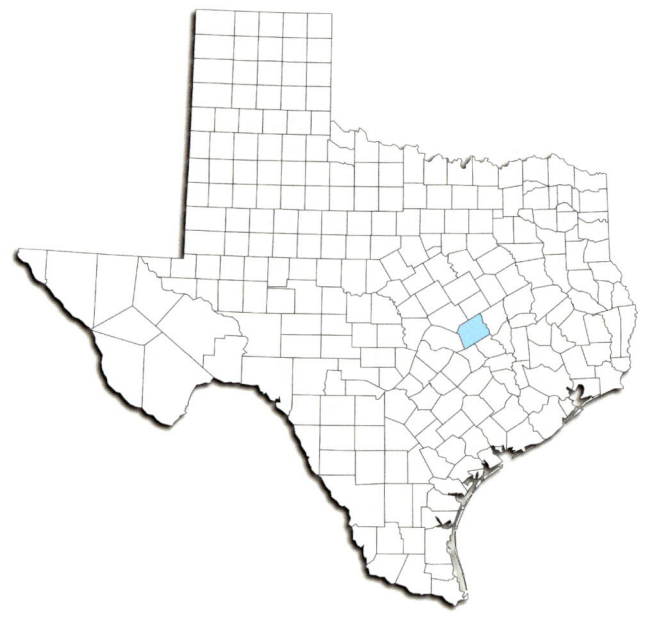

Created with paintmaps.com

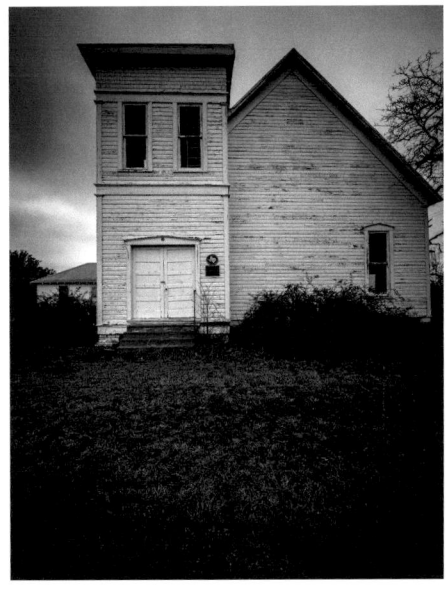

Front view of the main entrance.

Sharp, Texas, has always existed on the edges—never quite growing into a major town but never disappearing either. Like Rockdale and Clarkson, it was settled in the post-Civil War era by farmers drawn to the promise of rich land. The community grew around cotton, with a post office, a cotton gin, and small businesses springing up to support the agricultural economy.

By the early twentieth century, Sharp had reached its peak of 100 residents. The Sharp Presbyterian Church was established as a branch of an older congregation, a place for settlers to gather, celebrate, and mourn together. In many ways, the church was a symbol of the town's ambitions—it wasn't just a basic wooden structure, but one with Italianate architectural elements.

Sharp, like Clarkson, never grew into the bustling community that some had hoped. The cotton industry began to decline, and the rise of nearby urban centers pulled residents away. Today, Sharp is a quiet place, its population steady at around seventy-five people, far from the growth it once imagined.

And yet, the church remains. Now recognized as a Recorded Texas Historic Landmark, it stands not just as a piece of history but as a link between the past and present—a symbol of the settlers' belief that their town, and their faith, would endure.

Though these stories take place in different corners of Milam County, they are part of the same larger history. Rockdale, Clarkson, and Sharp were built on agriculture, shaped by the rise of industry, and challenged by the economic shifts that followed. The railroad brought prosperity, but changing times tested the resilience of those who called this land home.

The people of these towns—farmers, factory workers, immigrants, and pioneers—built lives around their communities, their work, and their churches. For many, faith was the one constant in an unpredictable world. When industries collapsed and populations declined, the churches became more than places of worship; they became historical markers, standing tall when so much else faded.

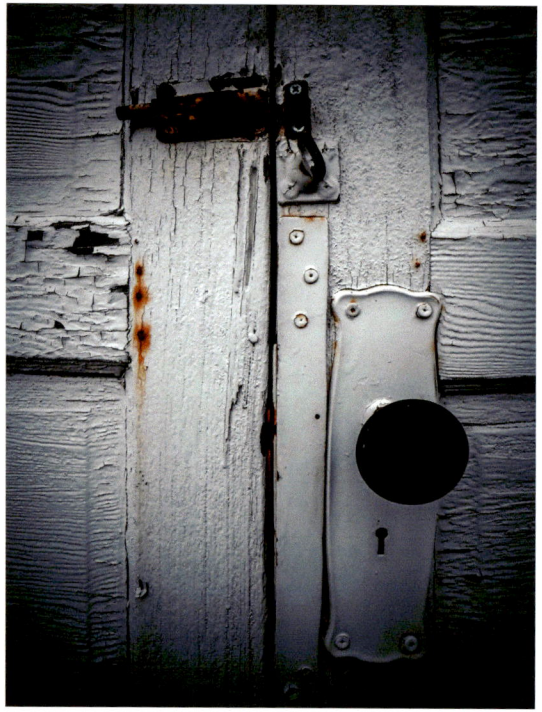

Close-up of intricate door latches.

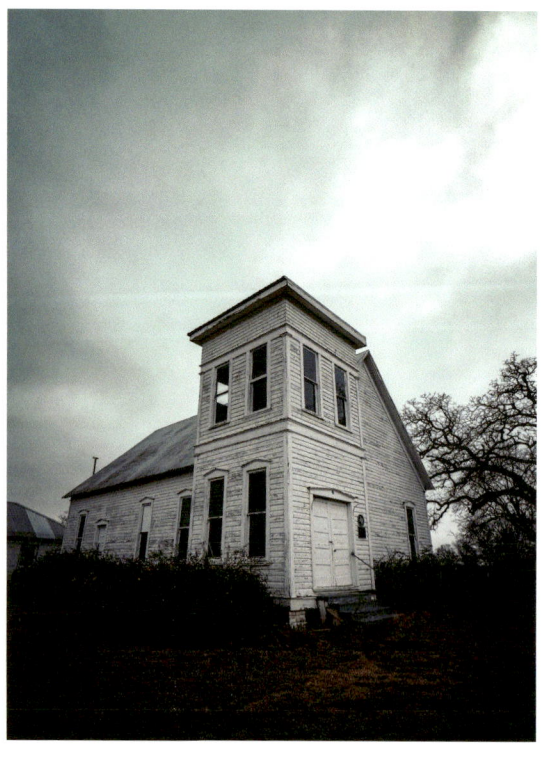

Modest exterior of Sharp Church.

7

Zion Apostolic Faith Mission Church: Angelina County, Rivercrest

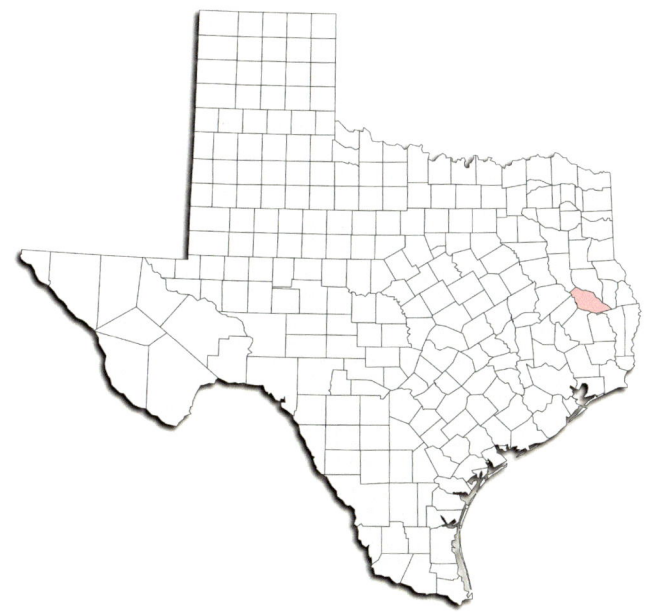

Created with paintmaps.com

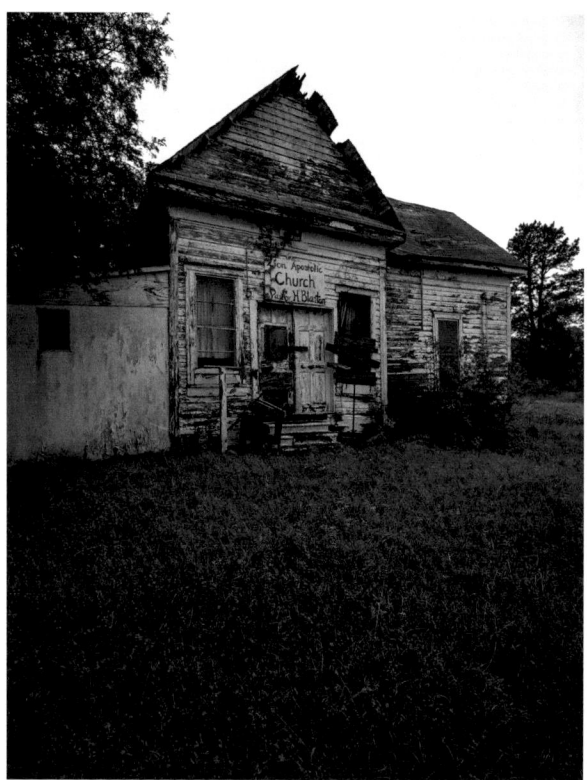

Zion Church exterior in Rivercrest.

There was a time when Rivercrest, Texas, felt like the perfect place to build a life. It was supposed to be a lakeside retreat, a community where families could enjoy the balance of rural charm and modern convenience. My grandfather saw it as that—a place where he could carve out a future for his family, where Thanksgiving was filled with the smoky scent of his deer sausage, and where memories were made against the backdrop of the pine trees and open sky.

But the dream that built Rivercrest was never fully realized. Due to a severe miscalculation, The Corps of Engineers failed to deliver on the lake, and what should have been a town centered around water and prosperity became one of unfinished roads and unfulfilled promises. Cut off from essential services, the community struggled to grow. Residents had to drive to Lufkin for basic needs, and with Precinct 2 providing little support, Rivercrest remained isolated, left to fend for itself.

The town's decline coincided with the hardships my family faced. Addiction, crime, and loss became an unavoidable reality. My uncle's battle with substance abuse ended with his body giving out too soon. My aunt's life was stolen over a drug debt, a senseless death that felt like an inevitability in a place where hope had long since faded. My grandfather, who had once been as strong as the land itself, spent his last years paying the price for a lifetime of drinking and smoking, confined to a bed as his body failed him.

Rivercrest is not just my family's story. It is the story of too many families who came here looking for something better, only to watch their dreams fall apart. Today, the town is defined by crime, addiction, and desperation. In a single year, the Angelina County Sheriff's Office responded to nearly 150 calls. In a neighborhood with only about 150 residents, according to the Texas Almanac, that statistic is staggering—calls ranging from domestic violence and drug-related disputes to even a triple murder. There are still people here who fight to make things better. Residents have built a sewage system and even a volunteer fire station, but without deed restrictions, homes fall into disrepair, and property values decline. It is a place where the fight for survival never stops.

Efforts have been made to improve infrastructure. A 2019 project sought to revamp the unit road system, but Rivercrest needs more than roads to change its fate. The town needs investment—police protection, emergency services, addiction recovery programs, and job training opportunities. It needs people to stop seeing it as a lost cause and start believing that places like Rivercrest are worth saving.

There is still a future here, if only someone is willing to fight for it.

Zion Church, now little more than a name in Rivercrest's fading history, remains an enigma. Its story is largely unknown—how active it once was, who worshipped there, or when its doors last opened. What is certain is that its presence, however small, once meant something to this struggling community. Now, like much of Rivercrest, it stands as a reminder of what has been lost.

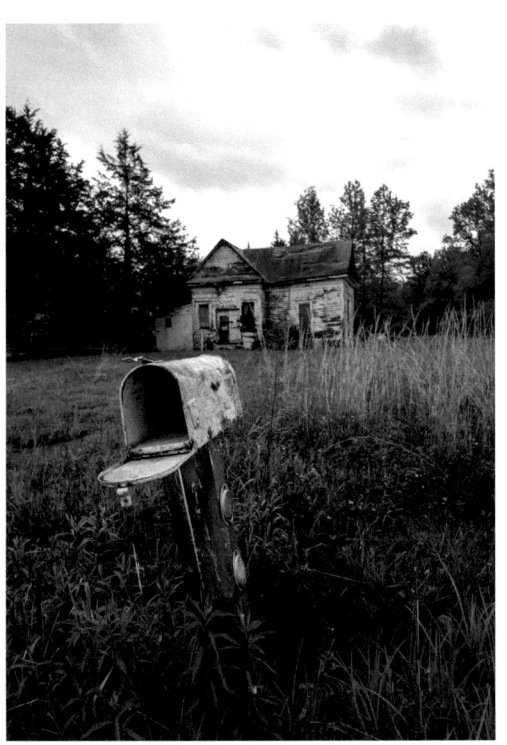 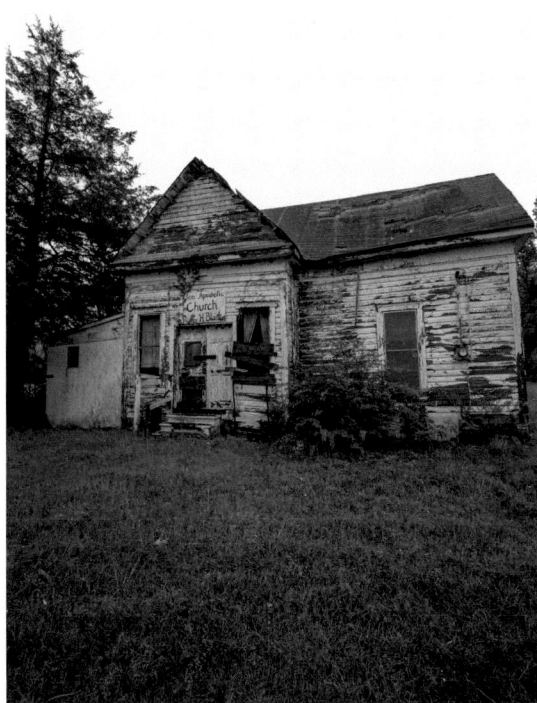

Above left: Forgotten Zion Church mailbox.

Above right: Boarded-up windows and doors.

8

Unknown Church:
Nacogdoches County, Etoile

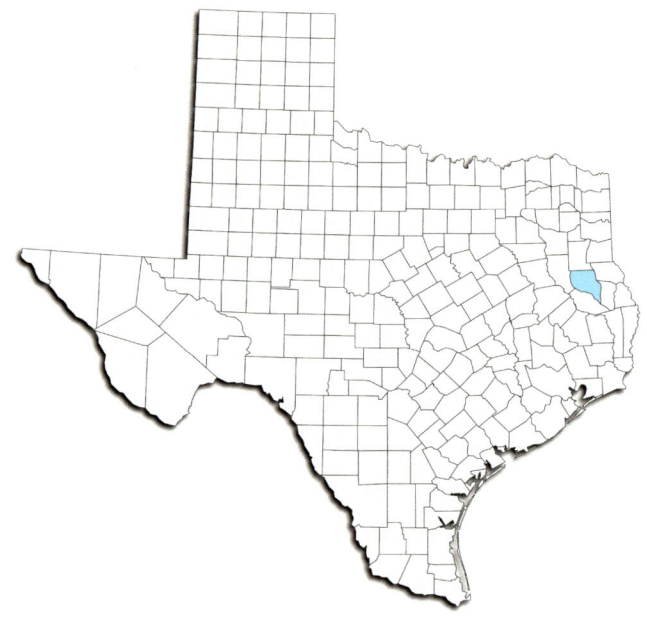

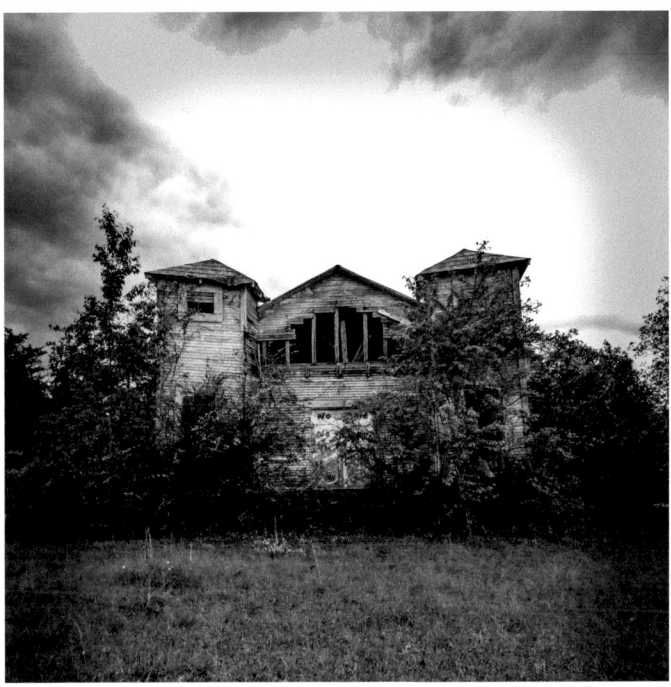

Silent, abandoned church in Etoile.

Not far from Rivercrest, across the county line in Nacogdoches, Etoile, Texas, tells a quieter but equally devastating story. There is no crime wave here, no frequent police calls, no headlines about triple murders. Instead, Etoile suffers in silence.

For decades, it was a town in slow decline. In the early 1900s, it was home to 300 people, with stores, a cotton gin, and a sense of community. But, much like Rivercrest, the world moved on without it. By the 1950s, only fifty people remained. The construction of Sam Rayburn Reservoir in the 1960s brought new life, turning Etoile into a quiet retirement community, but that was not enough to sustain it.

The greatest loss came in 2022, when the Etoile Independent School District was forced to close due to dwindling enrollment. What was once a proud community with its own schools, its own identity, was absorbed into Woden ISD. The loss of the school was not just a logistical problem—it was an emotional wound, as with churches, schools are the heart of small towns. They bring people together, they create memories, and they provide hope that the next generation will carry on what was built before them. With the school gone, Etoile became just another forgotten town.

But for those who remain, the struggle continues. Like Rivercrest, addiction has taken root here. The opioid crisis has hit rural Texas hard, and with so few resources available, many who need help will never get it. According to the Texas Health and Human Services Commission, Nacogdoches County has been classified as a Health Professional Shortage Area for mental health services. There are not enough doctors, not enough counselors, not enough treatment centers for the people who need them most.

At one time, a small church in Etoile provided some hope. It was a gathering place, a sanctuary for those struggling with addiction, a reminder that even in the hardest times,

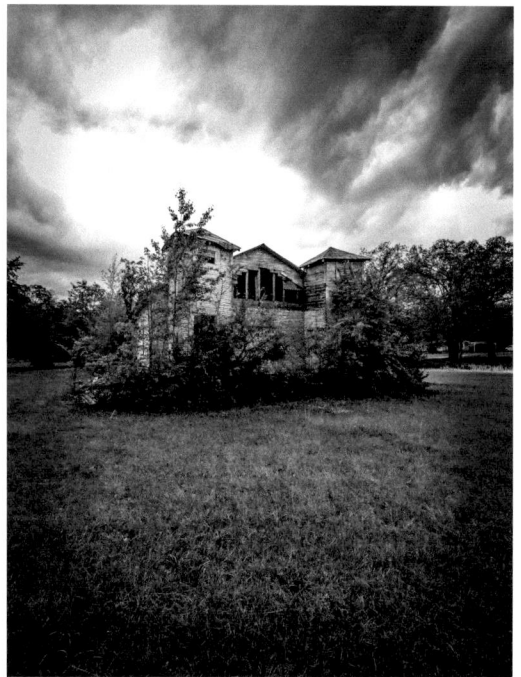 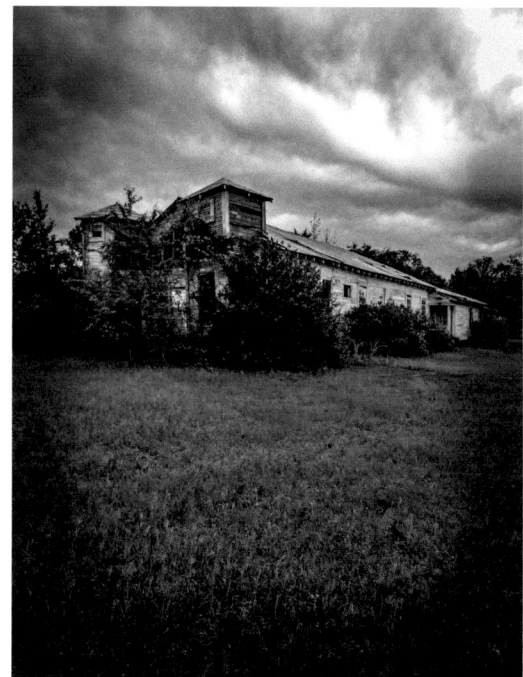

Above left: Wide-angle shot of the church exterior.

Above right: Flowering bushes behind the church.

faith could be a source of strength. But like the school, the church eventually closed its doors, another casualty of a town that had run out of people to keep it alive.

There are those who want to change things. Community leaders and healthcare advocates are pushing for expanded access to medication-assisted treatment, better funding for mental health services, and grassroots programs to support recovery. But these efforts are not enough without real government intervention.

The Trump administration's healthcare policies only make matters worse. Medicaid cuts slash funding for rural hospitals and addiction treatment programs. While some policies have attempted to expand opioid recovery services, the lack of funding has left communities like Etoile and Rivercrest without the resources they desperately need. Without proper healthcare access, these communities cannot break free from the cycle of addiction and poverty that has plagued them for generations.

Rivercrest and Etoile are two sides of the same coin. One fights loudly, drowning in crime and violence. The other fades quietly, suffocating under neglect. But both are victims of the same problem—a system that forgets about the places that don't seem worth saving.

But these places are worth saving. Rivercrest still has people willing to fight. Etoile still has people who remember what it used to be. There is still a way forward, if the right people are willing to listen.

9

Guadalupe El Torero Church: Hidalgo County, Linn

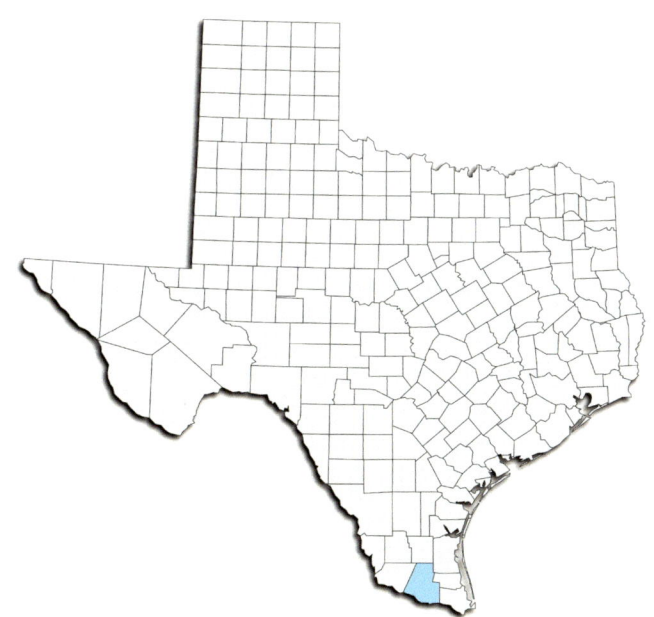

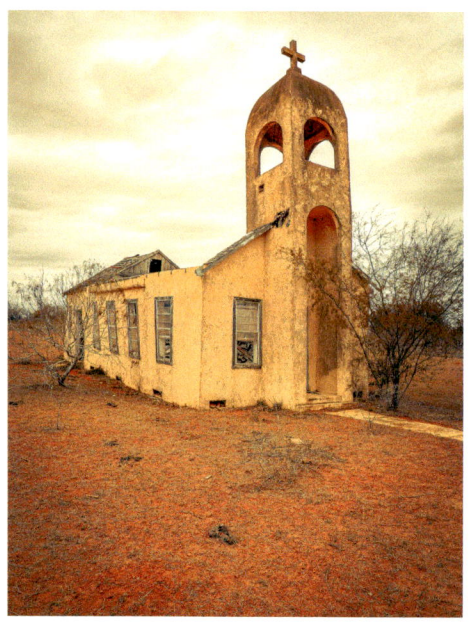

Caved roof with a precarious bell tower.

Linn, Texas, is named after John Joseph Linn, an Irish-born merchant and political figure in early Texas history. Born in 1798, he played a significant role in the Texas Revolution by supplying provisions, advocating for Texan independence, and serving as a delegate at the Convention of 1836. Linn was instrumental in the development of Victoria, Texas, and held political positions in the Republic of Texas government. A vocal critic of Mexican President Antonio López de Santa Anna, he opposed the centralization of power and authoritarian policies. While respected for his advocacy of Texan self-governance, Mexican authorities saw him as a political agitator.

The area that became Linn, Texas, was originally part of Spanish and Mexican land grants. It later developed as a small rural community due to its fertile land, attracting settlers in the nineteenth and twentieth centuries. Today, Linn remains a quiet, rural town with a predominantly Hispanic population of approximately 800.

Linn is governed by Hidalgo County, which has traditionally leaned Democratic, though recent elections have shown a growing Republican presence. While John Joseph Linn played a role in Texas' early history, the modern political landscape of the area has evolved independently of his influence. Today, the community faces typical rural challenges, including economic development, infrastructure improvement, and access to education and healthcare

Land grants, large tracts of land distributed by the Spanish Crown, the Mexican government, and later the Republic and State of Texas, were issued to settlers, empresarios, and military veterans to encourage colonization, reward service, and develop communities. These grants laid the foundation for land ownership in Texas, reinforcing the principle that all land must be owned.

This concept of land ownership stems from both legal and economic frameworks established throughout Texas history. Under Spanish and Mexican rule, land was

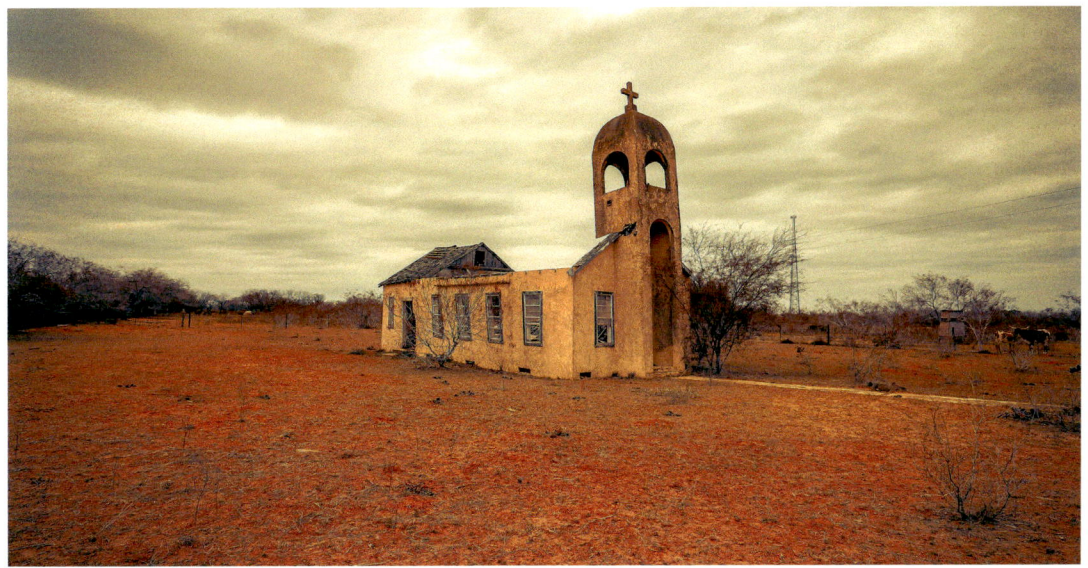

Cows roaming near the church.

granted with the expectation that it would be settled, developed, and contribute to the economy. When Texas became independent and later joined the United States, private land ownership was further solidified through property laws that required land to have a legal owner to ensure taxation, development, and orderly governance.

In Texas, as in much of the United States, land ownership is tied to property rights, economic productivity, and local governance. Privately held land contributes to infrastructure development, agriculture, and commerce, while public lands are managed for conservation, recreation, and resource extraction. The idea that all land must be owned—whether privately, by the state, or federally—ensures that it is accounted for, utilized effectively, and protected from disputes over control or abandonment.

The story of the Guadalupe El Torero Church begins on January 5, 1924, when Juan Cavazos, a local landowner, acquired 10 acres from the San Ramon Land Grant. This grant was originally part of a larger tract given to Julian Farias by King Carlos III of Spain in 1791.

Architectural styles like Spanish Colonial and Mexican adobe were predominant during the nineteenth century due to the area's climate and available supplies. These structures showcase the practical methods used by early settlers, such as adobe brickmaking, which involves mixing clay, water, and straw, and wooden beam construction using locally harvested timber.

Cavazos, aiming to support his community's spiritual needs, donated land for a church, which was built under Father Gustavo Goldbach. The church, with its simple yet charming architecture, featured an entry tower, celestial blue trim, wooden benches, and plank floors. Its windows offered peaceful views of grazing cattle, adding to its rustic charm. Over time, the church fell into disuse and disrepair, becoming a cherished but deteriorating relic for many locals, who fondly remembered attending services there as a child.

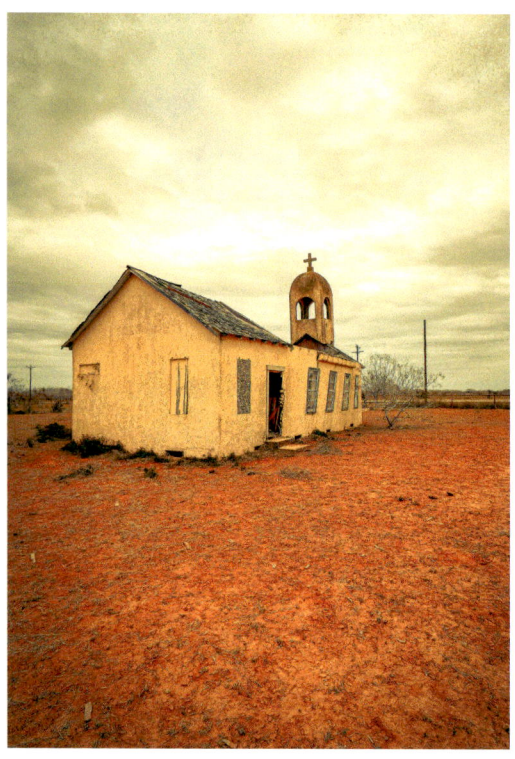

Left: Rear view showing disrepair.

Below left: Tree growing in front of the church.

Below right: Bell tower hanging precariously.

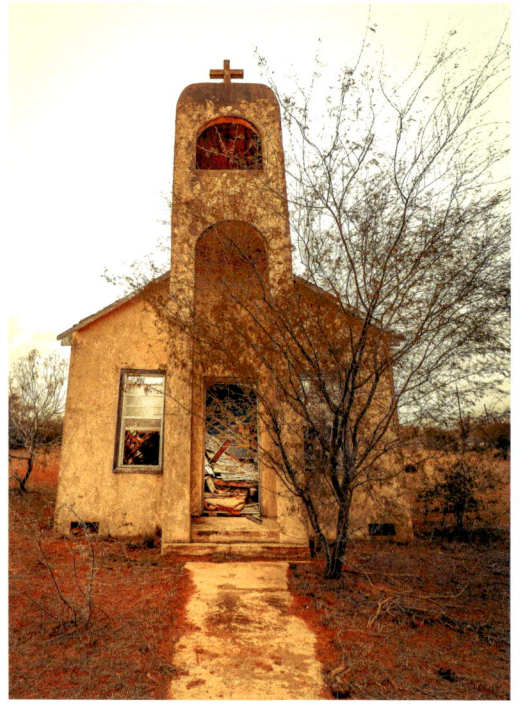

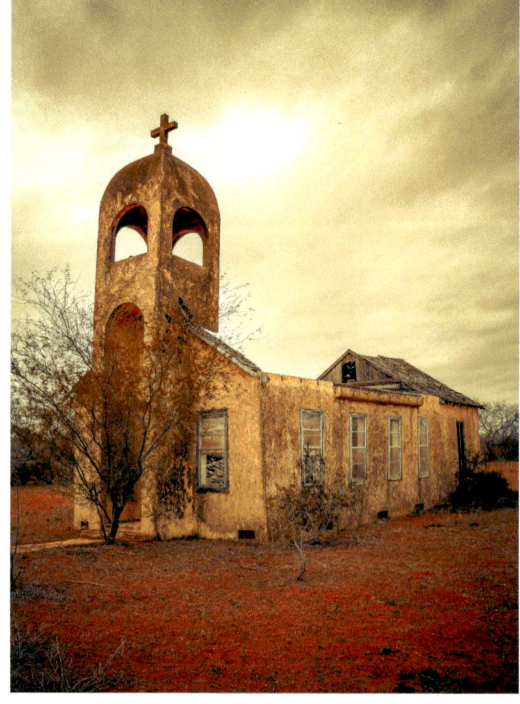

The situation changed dramatically in July 2020 when Hurricane Hanna struck the region. The powerful hurricane caused extensive damage to the already fragile church, leading to its destruction. The loss of the church was a significant blow to the community, which had long valued the building as a historical and spiritual landmark.

In the wake of the hurricane's devastation, Linn's community rallied to rebuild their cherished church. Spearheaded by local figures like Sylvia Perez Kotzur, a fundraising campaign was launched to construct a new church on the original site. The goal was to preserve the historical charm of the old church while incorporating modern features for durability. The community's dedication to honoring their heritage was evident in every aspect of the project. Now completed, the new church continues to serve as a place of worship and community gathering, upholding its legacy of faith and cultural significance.

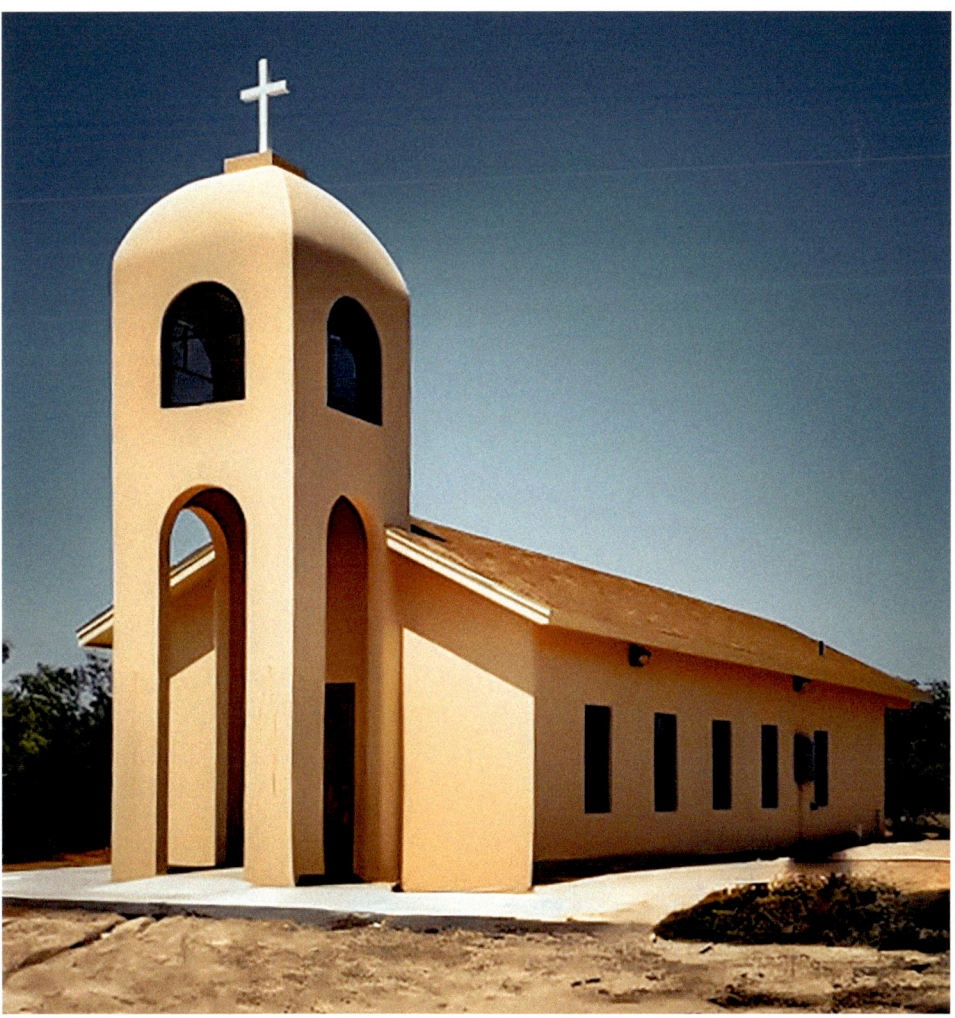

Recently restored Lin church.

10

First Methodist Church:
Jack County, Jermyn

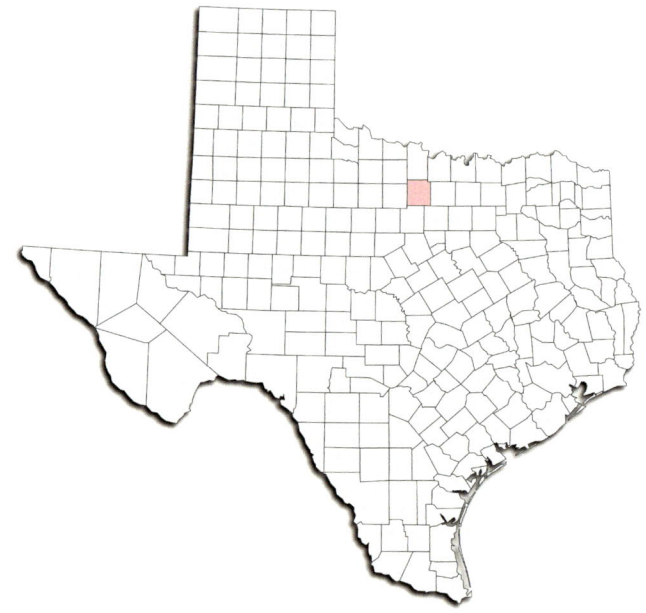

Created with paintmaps.com

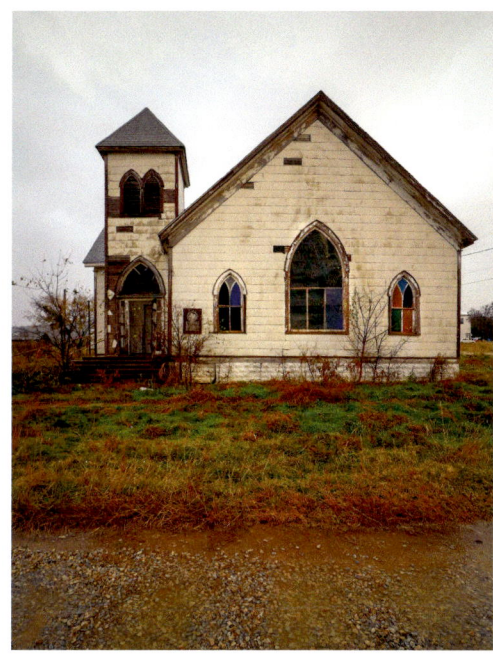

Outside view of the church.

Jermyn, Texas, founded in 1909 in Jack County, was named after John Joseph Jermyn, a key figure in developing and president of the Gulf, Texas and Western Railways. This railroad was crucial for the town's growth, supporting trade and movement. Early development was fueled by agriculture and oil, leading to the construction of vital infrastructure. As the community grew and thrived, so did the need for a dedicated place of worship that would reflect the values and aspirations of its residents.

The First Methodist Church congregation initially met in homes and temporary spaces, united by a strong sense of community and Methodist values. The first permanent church building was completed in 1912, showcasing Gothic Revival architectural elements characterized by its pointed arches, decorative trim, and stained-glass windows. These design choices were influenced by the desire to create spaces that inspired awe and reflection among congregants.

Stepping inside, I was met with an atmosphere where the beauty of the stained glass mingled with the weight of decay. Sunlight filtered through the vibrant windows, casting a kaleidoscope of colors—rich blues, deep greens, and warm ambers—across the worn wooden pews. A play of light and color illuminated the sanctuary, evoking a sense of tranquility and reverence that enhanced the overall spiritual ambiance of the space.

The church's once-elegant ceiling now features a patchwork of wooden panels, adding a rustic charm. Navigating the scattered debris, the chipped crosses on the doors, and the weathered interior evoked a palpable sense of connection to its history.

This combination of beauty and neglect created a deeply emotional experience. Every detail, from the intricate stained glass to the aging pews, and the ever-present piano—always left behind because who wants to move that?—tells a story of hope, faith, and the enduring spirit of those who came before.

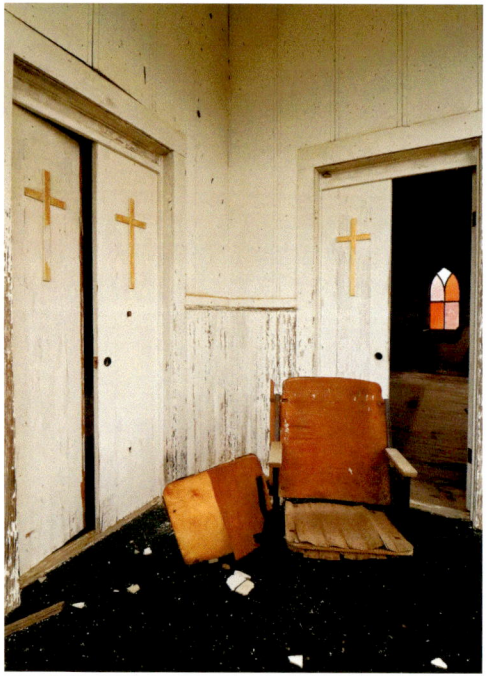

Entrance door craftsmanship close-up.

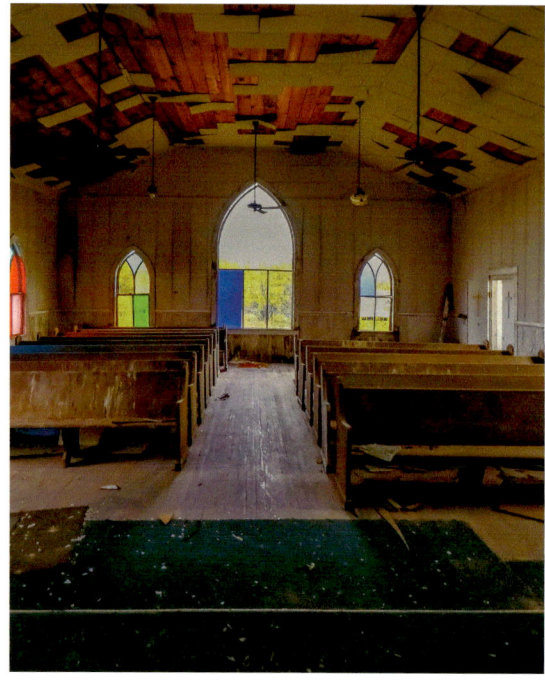

View from the altar towards the back of the church.

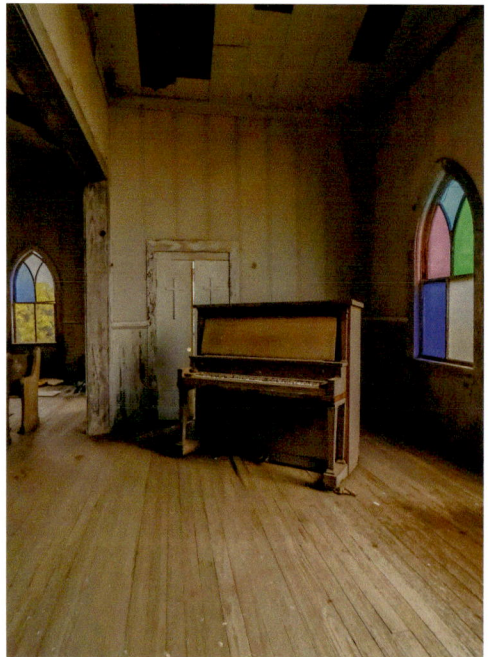

Abandoned piano left behind.

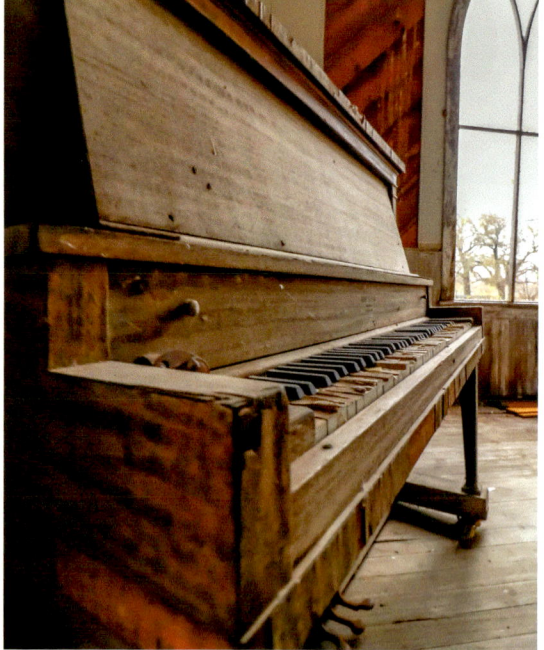

Full view of the bulky piano.

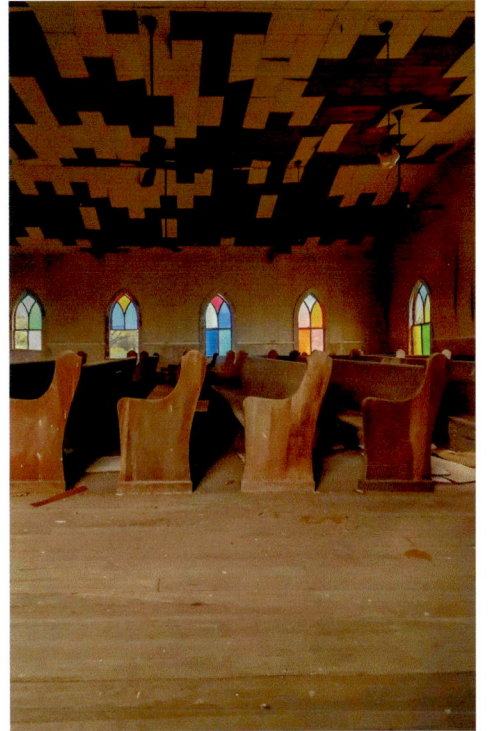

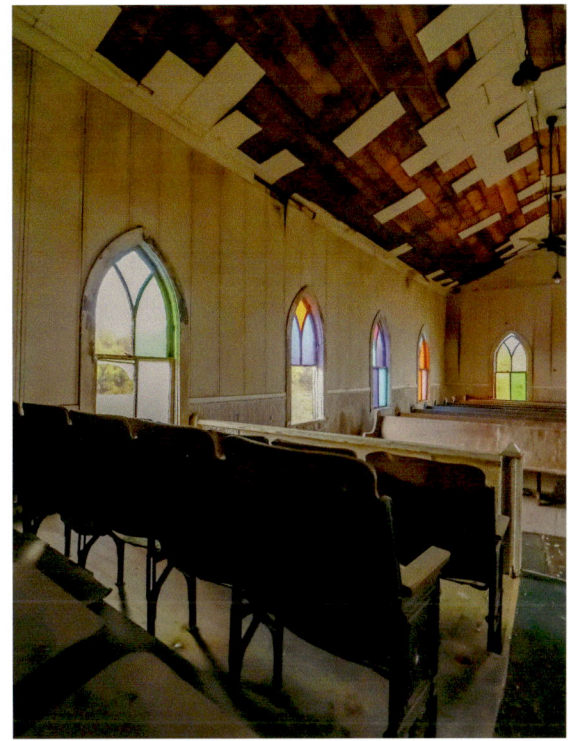

Above left: Lined pews with stunning stained glass.

Above right: Shot from behind the choir pews.

Right: Nature reclaiming the church.

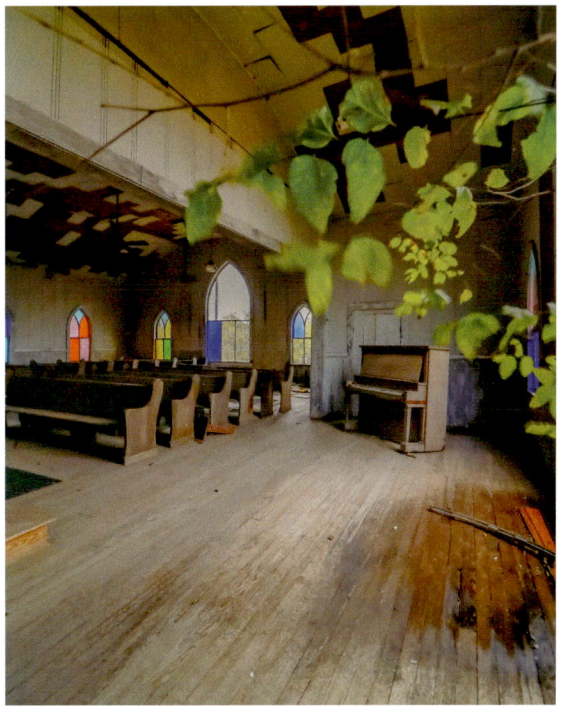

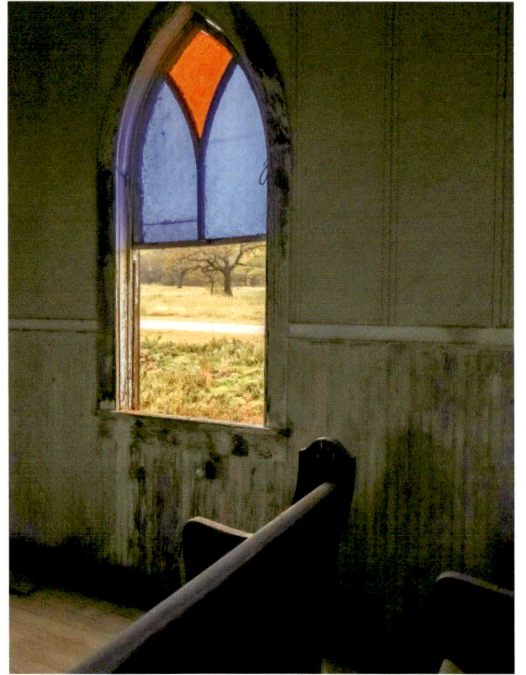

Close-up of stained glass.

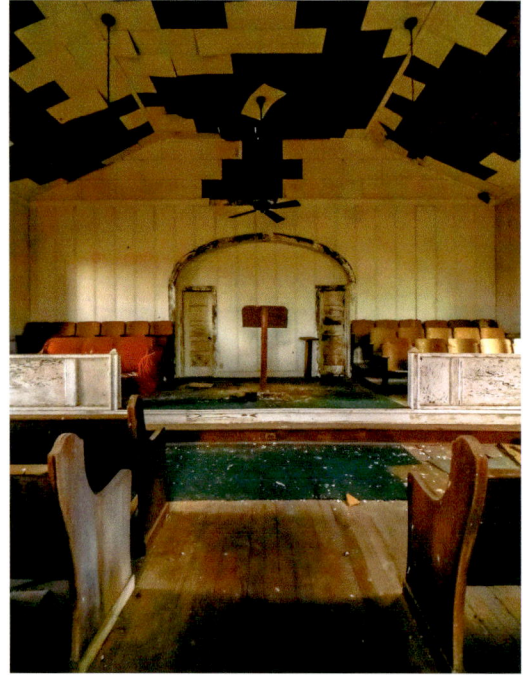

View toward the altar.

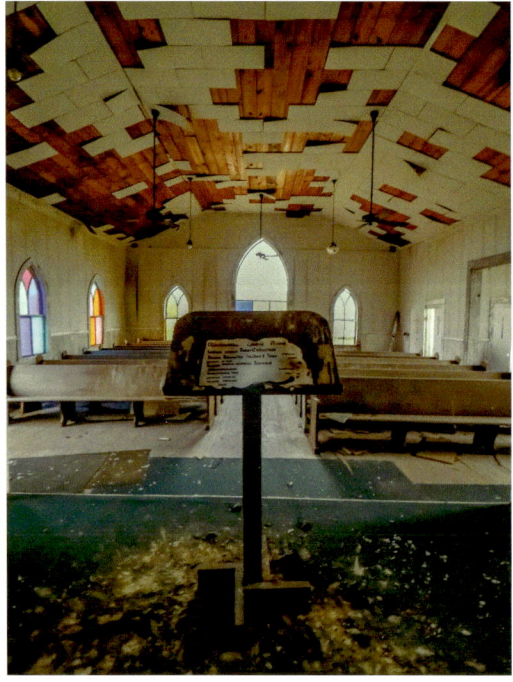

Audience view from the altar.

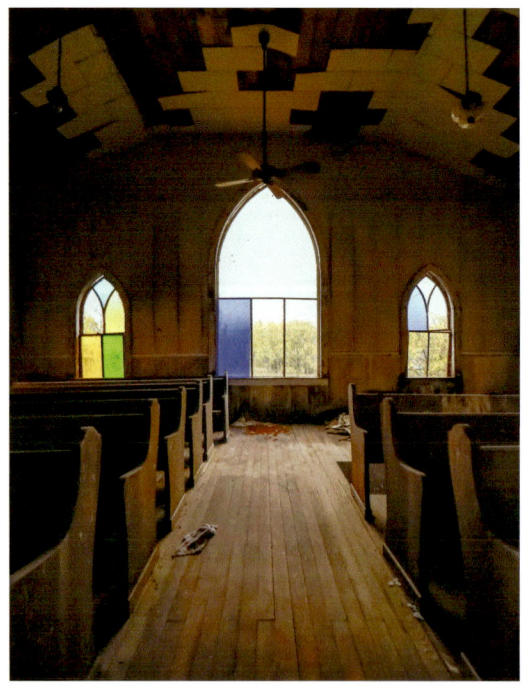

Middle aisle view of stained glass.

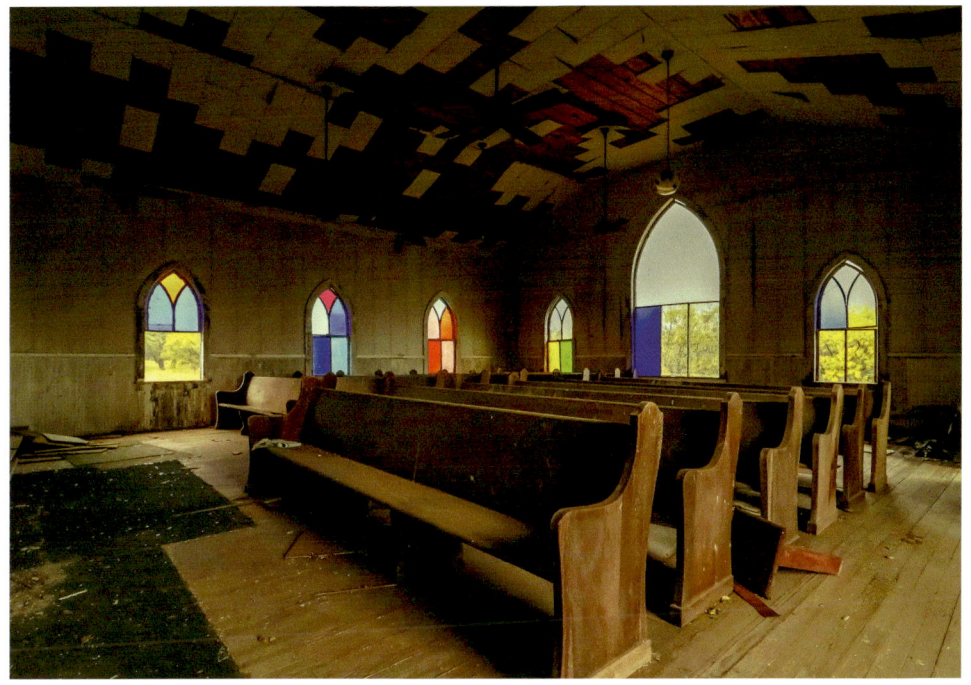

Worn pews and stained glass.

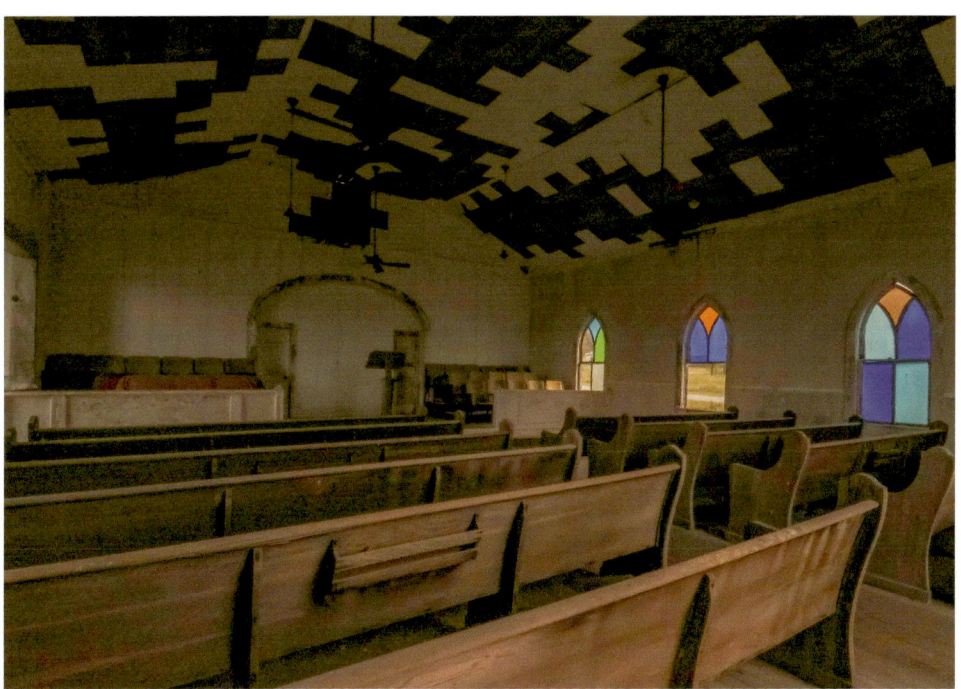

Central area with beautiful windows.

11

The Bartlett First Presbyterian Church: Bell County & Williamson County, Bartlett

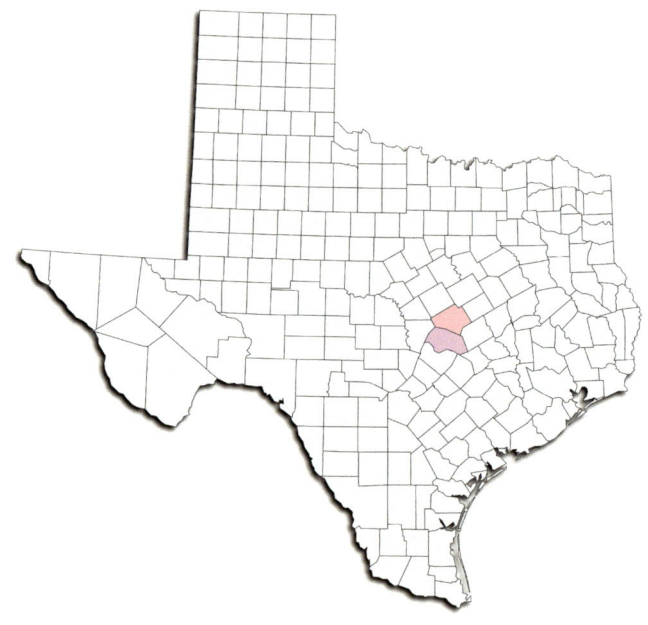

Created with paintmaps.com

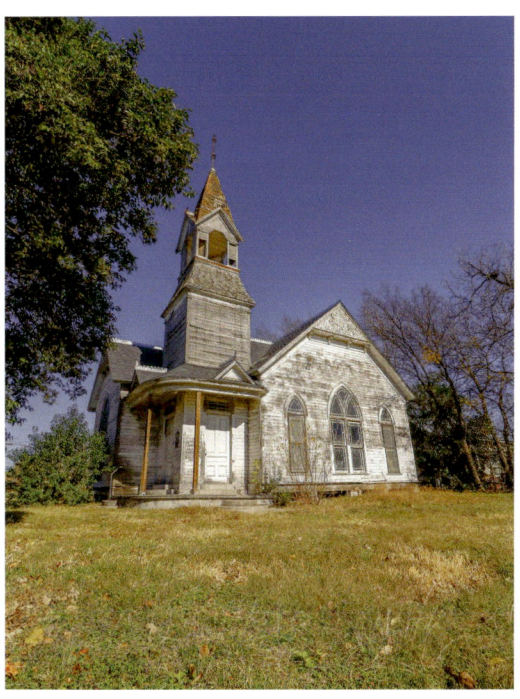

Bartlett Church from a low angle.

Bartlett, Texas, like other towns in early Texas, began attracting settlers in the 1850s due to its fertile land and economic opportunities. The town was formally established in 1882 when the Missouri, Kansas, and Texas Railroad extended its line through the area, spurring rapid development. Bartlett uniquely spans two counties, Bell and Williamson, which can complicate service management but also provides resources from both.

This dual-county situation arose from historical land grants and the development of transportation routes like railroads, which often crossed county lines. Bartlett's history includes significant growth and transformation, heavily influenced by its religious institutions. For example, the Bartlett First Presbyterian Church has been a landmark throughout the town's history.

In Bartlett, as in many frontier towns, churches were among the first community structures, serving as worship, social, and educational centers. Early settlers brought diverse religious traditions, leading to the establishment of several churches that played crucial roles in shaping the community's social and cultural life.

The Bartlett First Presbyterian Church quickly became a cornerstone of the Bartlett community. The original building, constructed in 1899 was a modest structure. As the congregation grew, so did the church's physical presence and influence within the community.

The church underwent several renovations and expansions throughout the twentieth century. A significant remodel in the 1920s added Gothic Revival architectural elements, enhancing its aesthetic appeal and making it a prominent landmark in Bartlett. These changes resulted from the congregation's growing prosperity, and the economic boom Bartlett experienced during this period.

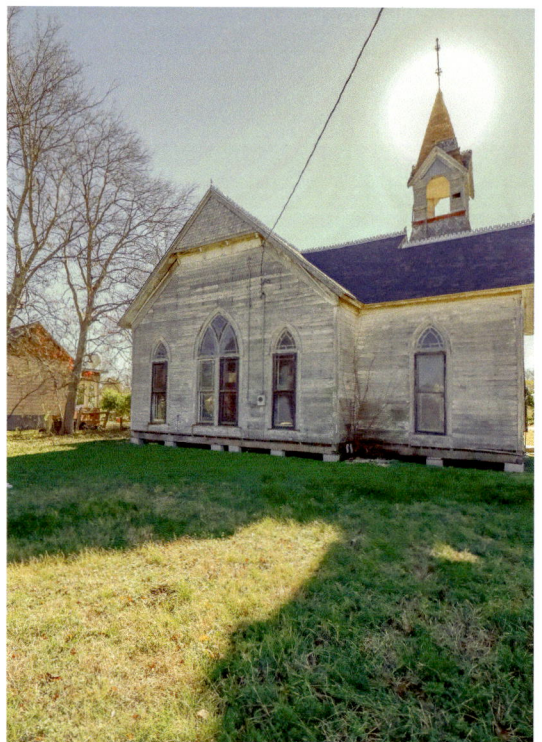

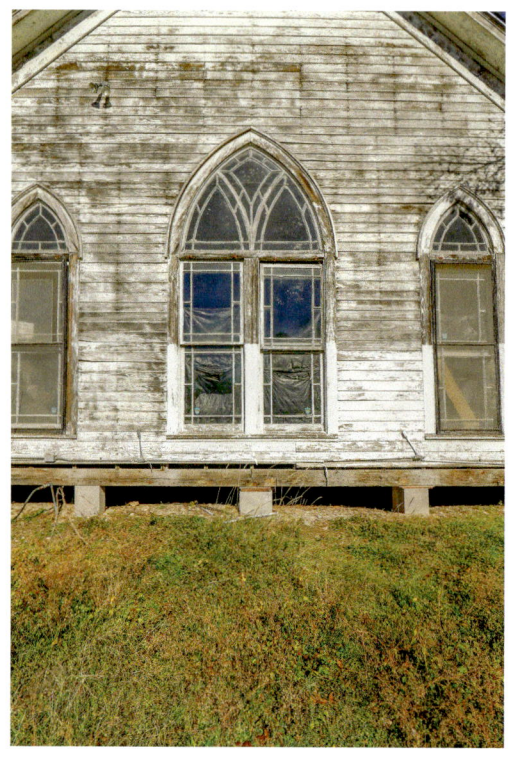

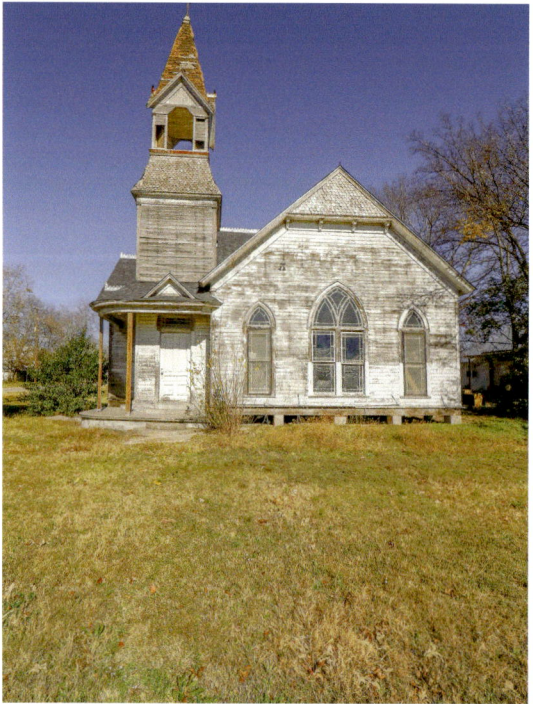

Above left: Rear view highlighting structure.

Above right: Close-up of detailed window.

Left: Bartlett Church exterior.

Bartlett faced significant economic challenges in the late twentieth century, like other early Texas towns, primarily due to declining agricultural viability, limited economic diversification, and a shrinking population. Like many of the other rural areas we have explored, as young residents moved to urban areas in search of better opportunities, the community's vitality diminished, impacting local institutions like the Bartlett First Presbyterian Church. Attendance dropped significantly, and as economic hardships persisted, the church fell into disrepair.

In 2017, a preservation enthusiast bought the church to restore it, but a fire in 2019 tragically destroyed the recently renovated building which enacted the need for better fire prevention and maintenance of historic structures. In the early 2020s, a new owner purchased what remained of the church, aiming to transform its Gothic Revival architecture into a unique living space. This effort is part of a movement to rejuvenate Bartlett's historic buildings and preserve the town's cultural heritage and attract tourists.

The renovation aimed to preserve the original structure and character of the Bartlett First Presbyterian Church while making it suitable for modern living. Significant structural work was done, including reinforcing the foundation, repairing the roof, and stabilizing walls. High ceilings and large windows of the Gothic Revival architecture were preserved, with the sanctuary converted into a spacious living area and the altar serving as a unique focal point.

Modern plumbing, electrical systems, and HVAC were installed, along with a new kitchen and bathroom for comfort and functionality. Original features like wooden

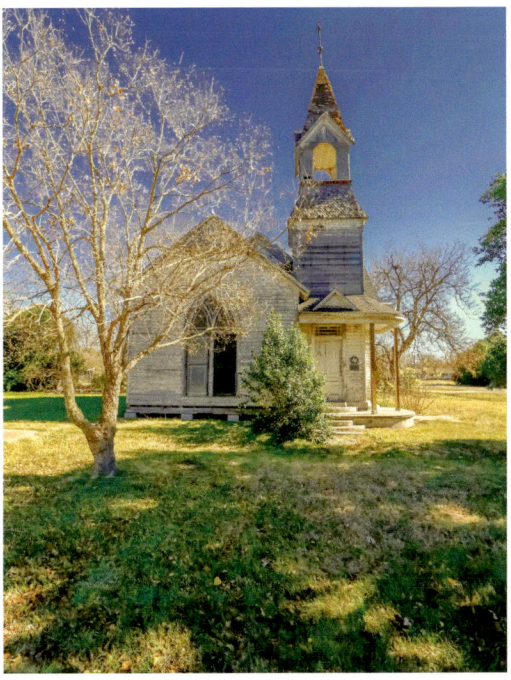 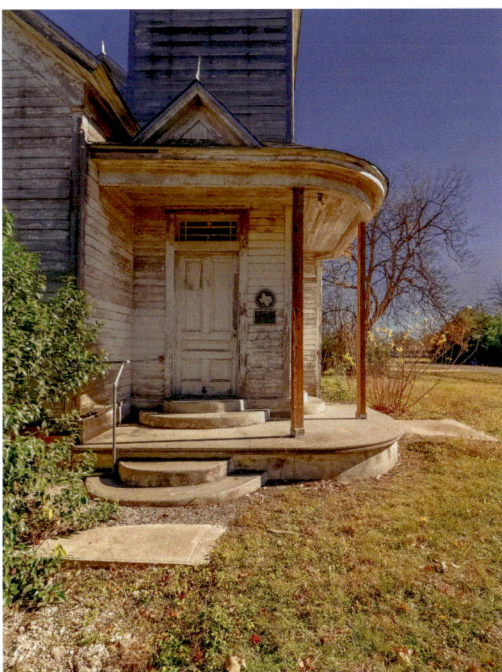

Above left: Classic architecture of Bartlett Church.

Above right: Unique curved front entrance.

pews, and flooring were restored and repurposed, adding charm to the living space. The transformation into a one-bedroom rental loft aligns with the growing trend of creating unique Airbnb's in even the most rural parts of the country. This trend has brought both benefits and consequences; while it boosts the local economy by attracting new visitors and residents, it also raises concerns about the potential for gentrification, a process by which historically lower-income neighborhoods experience rising property values and an influx of wealthier residents, often leading to the displacement of long-time residents and cultural change.Additionally, the sudden influx of visitors poses questions about safety and whether small towns like Bartlett are adequately prepared to handle increased traffic and the demands of tourists. As local infrastructure and services may be limited, ensuring the community can accommodate this growth while maintaining safety and quality of life for residents becomes crucial.

Converting the church into a rental space positively impacted the community, helping to preserve the town's architectural heritage while encouraging a new flow of tourism that revitalizes local businesses and promotes connections among residents and visitors alike.

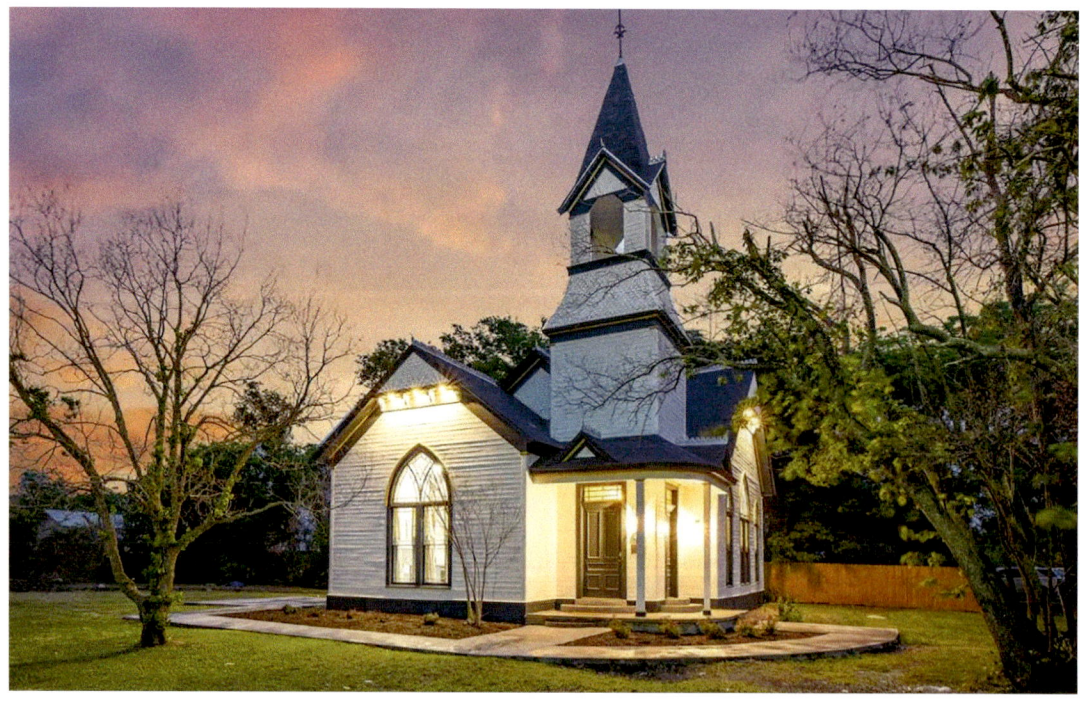

Restored church for travelers. (*Source: Airbnb*)

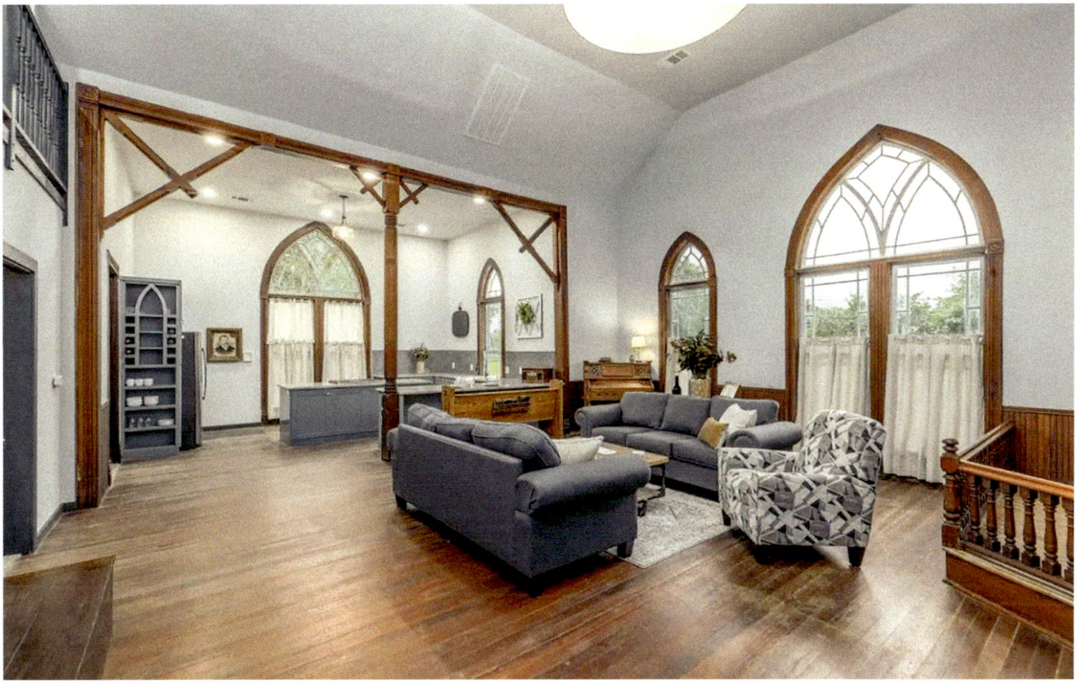

Historic windows in restored interior. (*Source: Airbnb*)

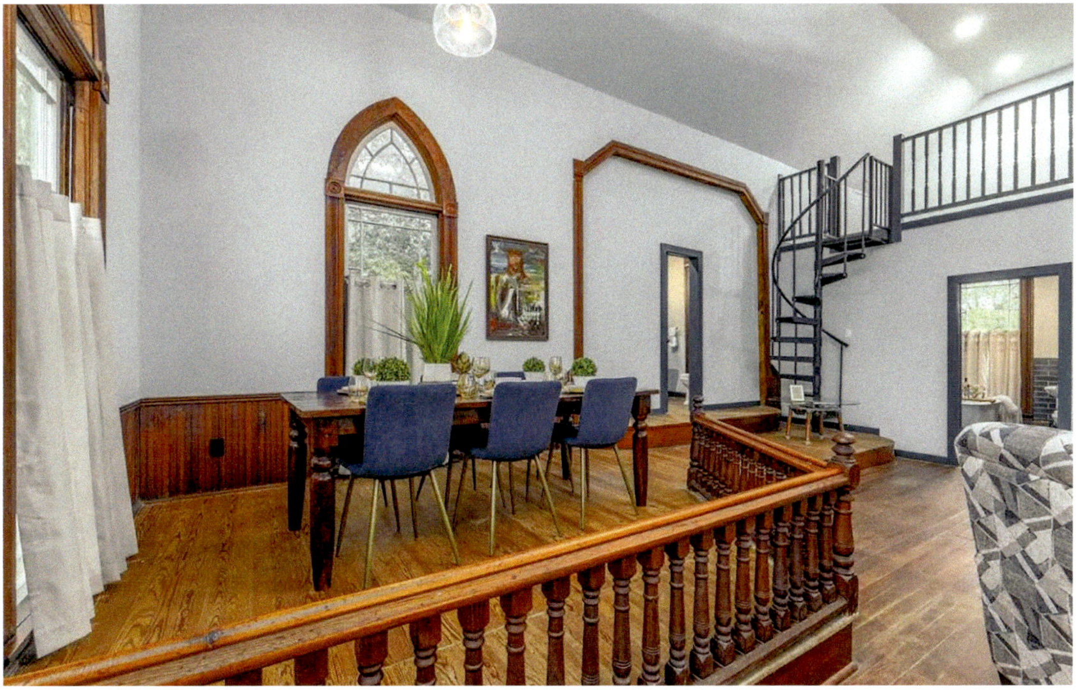

Blending history with modern design. (*Source: Airbnb*)

12

Old Second Baptist Church:
Nueces County, Corpus Christi

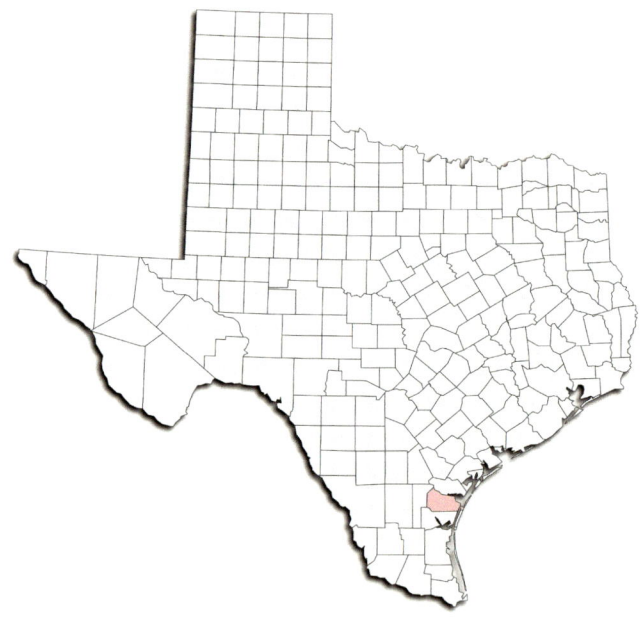

Created with paintmaps.com

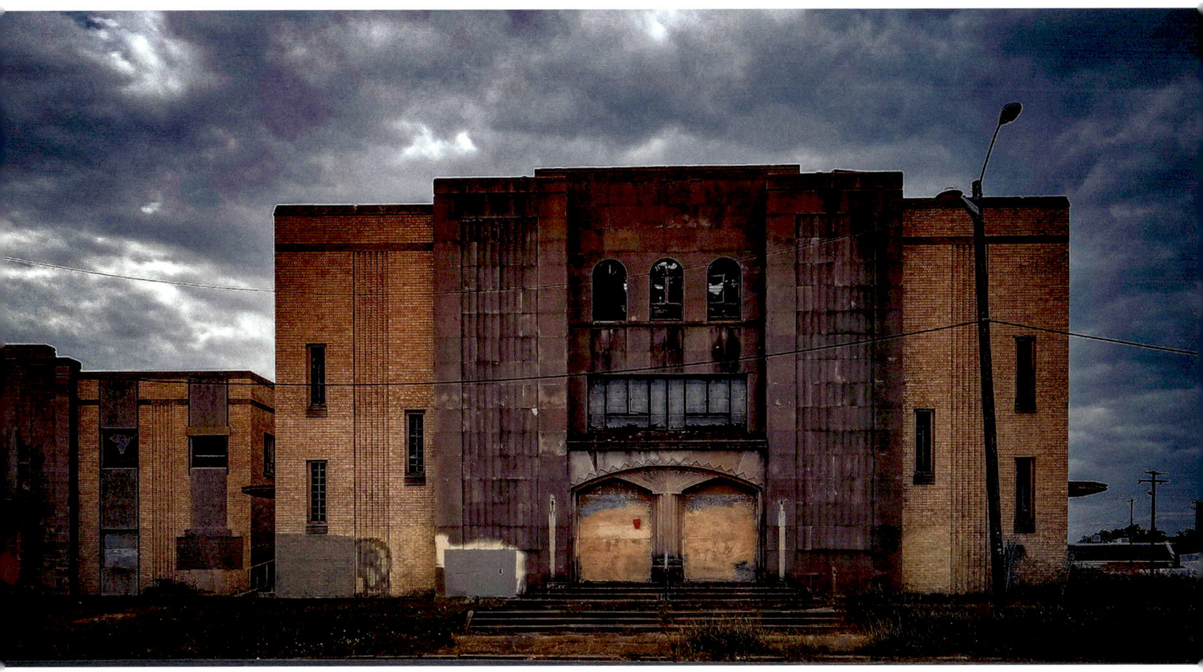

Exterior with unique design.

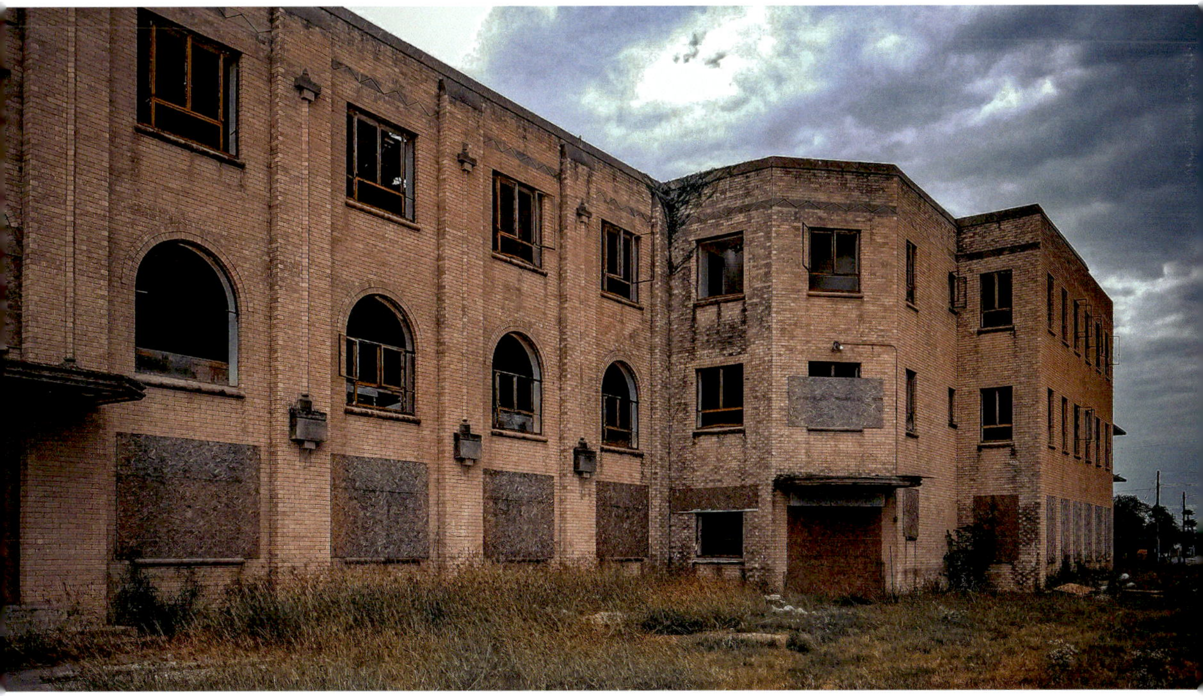

Side exterior shot.

Traveling south to Nueces County, I arrived at the Old Second Baptist Church in Corpus Christi, where signs of gentrification were evident. Research revealed that the Staples and Leopard corridors revitalization aims to rejuvenate Uptown Corpus Christi by attracting new businesses and investments. This initiative will create jobs, stimulate economic activity, and transform the area into a vibrant hub. Planned upgrades include better roads, street lighting, public transportation, and green spaces, all designed to enhance safety, accessibility, and quality of life, while attracting new residents and boosting local commerce.

As the neighborhood transforms, rising property values can benefit property owners with increased returns and higher tax revenues for further improvements. However, this also risks displacing long-time residents who cannot afford the higher costs. The demolition of historic sites like the Old Second Baptist Church highlights the issue of displacement, as rising rents push out lower-income families and disrupt communities. Additionally, the influx of new businesses and wealthier residents can shift the neighborhood's cultural identity, threatening long-standing local businesses and altering the area's unique character. Balancing modernization with cultural preservation is crucial to maintaining the neighborhood's distinct identity.

Gentrification can heighten social tensions between new and existing residents, with economic divides leading to resentment among those displaced. To address these issues, inclusive community planning and affordable housing initiatives are essential. Community meetings and forums provide platforms for residents to voice concerns and influence development plans, striving for more equitable benefits from gentrification.

The Old Second Baptist Church played an integral role in the spiritual life of its congregation. With its rich history, the church provided not only a space for religious services but also promoted community connections through educational programs and social gatherings. In 1944, the original building suffered significant damage from a fire, prompting the congregation to vote to rename the church and invest in a new structure. The newly constructed church, completed in 1944, cost an excess of $400,000, and included both a main church and a fellowship building, emphasizing the congregation's commitment to both worship and community outreach. However, as the uptown community changed, the church faced challenges adapting to its evolving

By the mid-1980s, Second Baptist Church had relocated to a new home on the south side of Corpus Christi, leaving behind its original building. Over the ensuing decades, the structure changed hands multiple times but remained primarily abandoned. The former church and school complex, which had once echoed with hymns and laughter, now faced an uncertain future.

Early in my career, I stumbled upon this hidden gem, marking one of my most unforgettable explorations. While some adventures serve as valuable lessons, and others are defined by awkward or unsettling moments, exploring the Old Second Baptist Church felt like stepping into a tangible reflection of Corpus Christi's downtown district's current phase.

The lighting in the building was surreal; shadows and sunlight danced through the broken windows, with golden rays casting intricate patterns on the dusty floors. Some rooms were softly illuminated, creating an ethereal atmosphere, while others were bathed in intense light, revealing every detail.

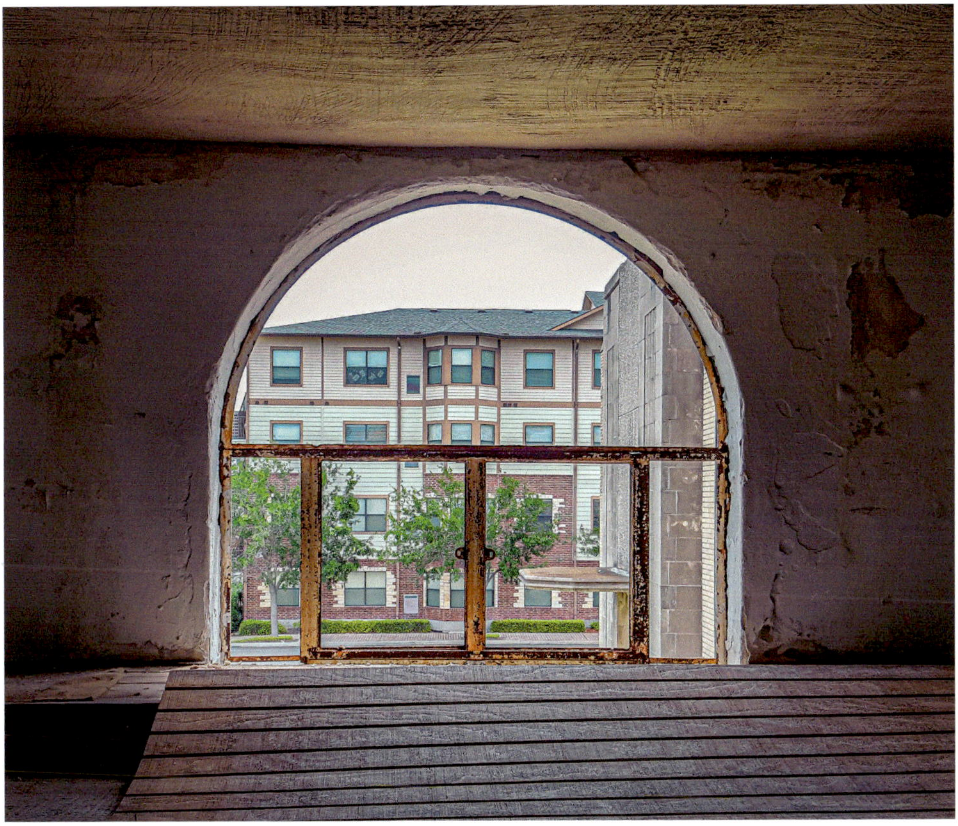

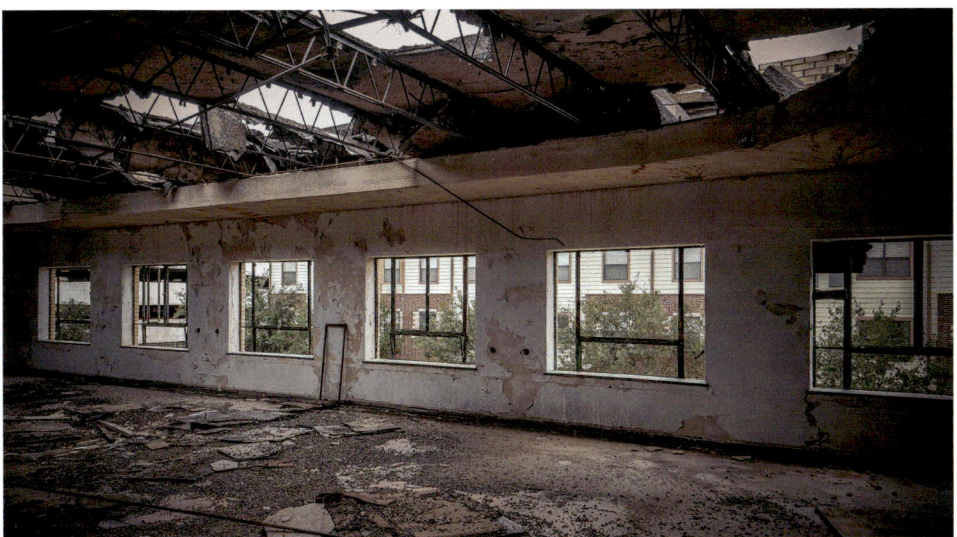

Gentrification's old *v*. new contrast.

Lined windows with gentrification view.

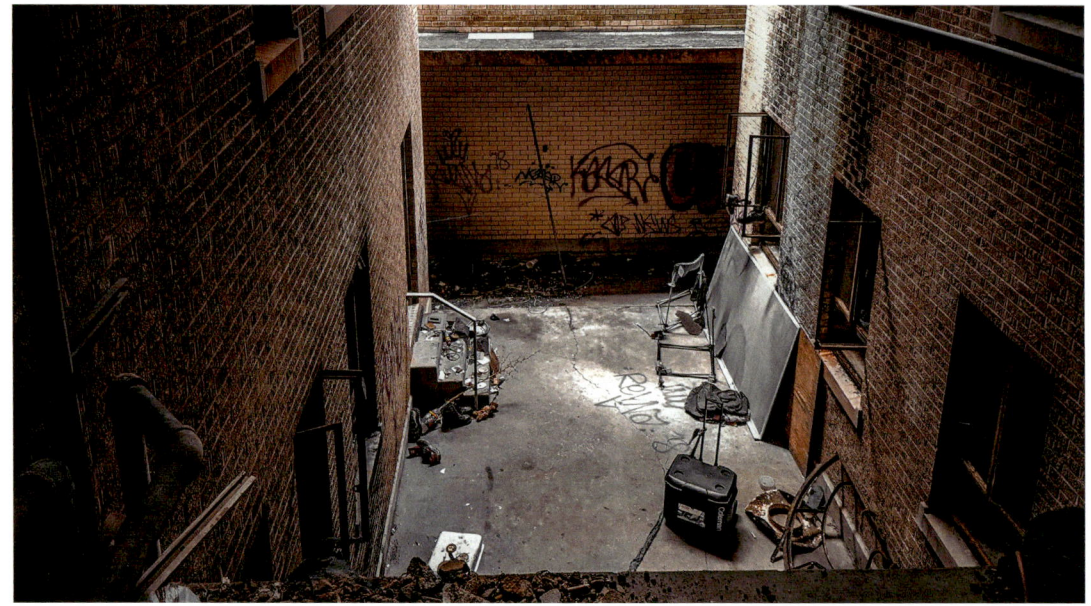

Open-air alley overtaken by squatters.

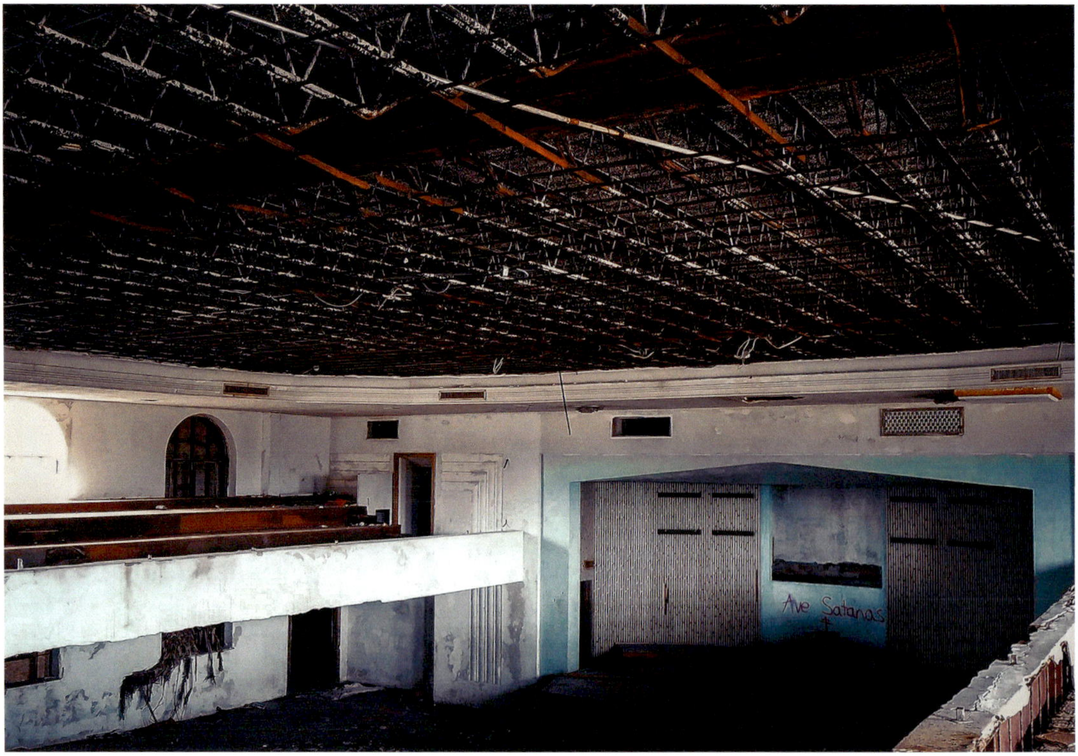

Stage view from second level.

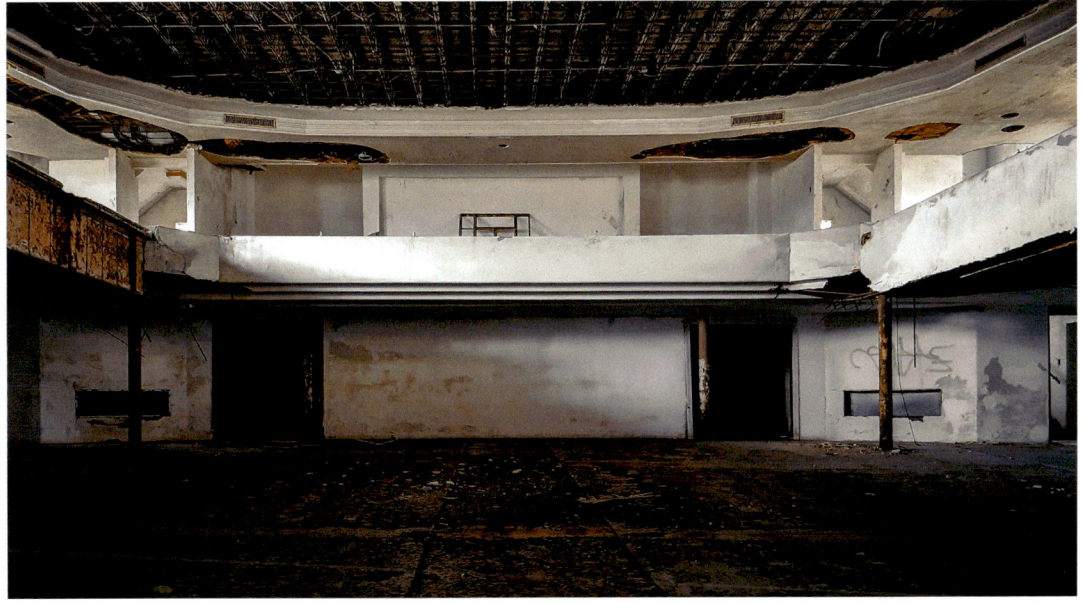

Wrap-around seating from the stage.

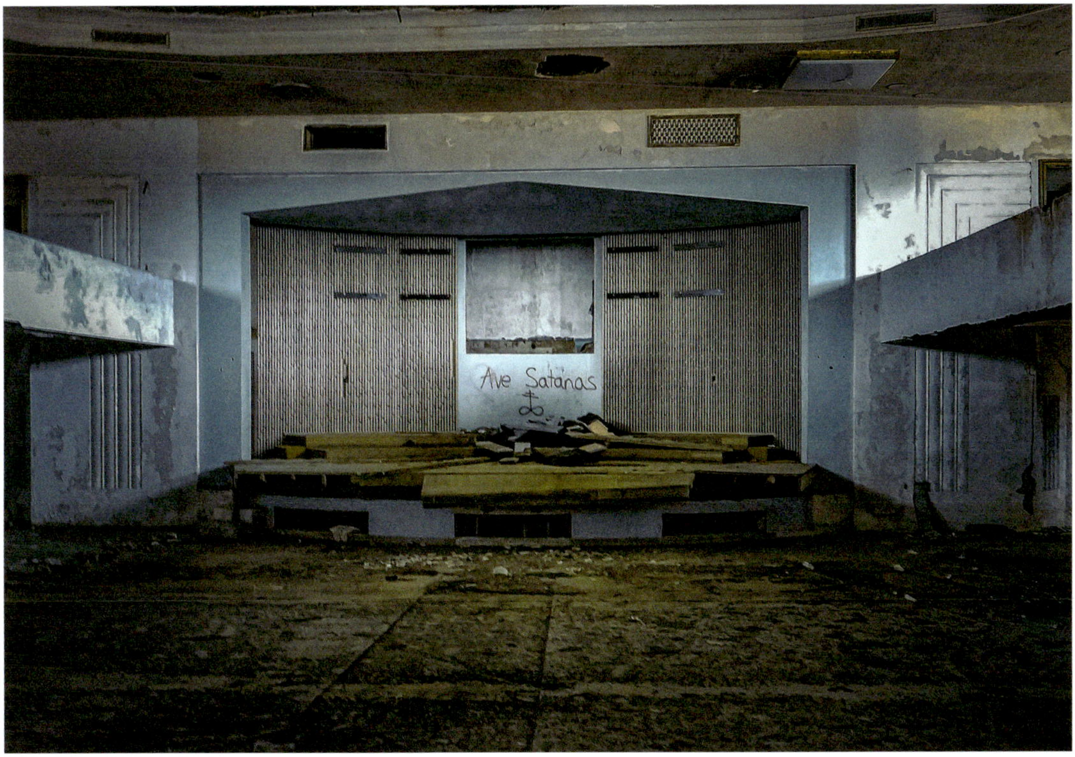

Ground-level view of the main stage.

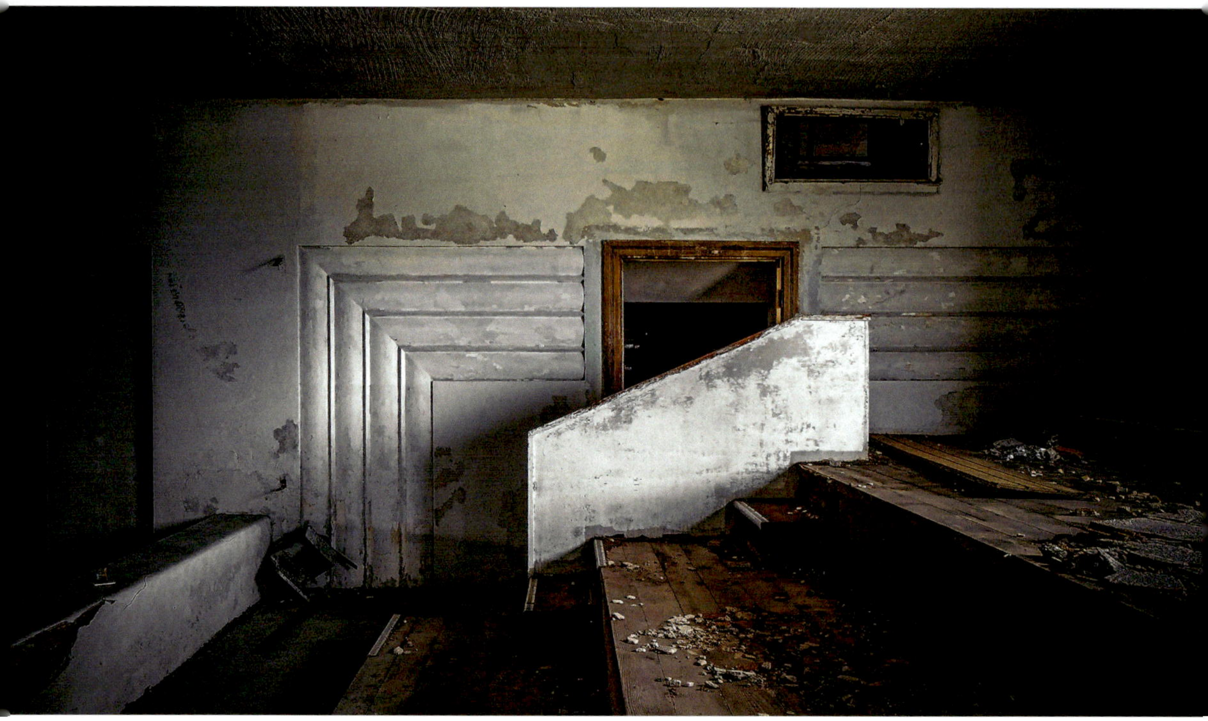

Upper deck view of the stairwell.

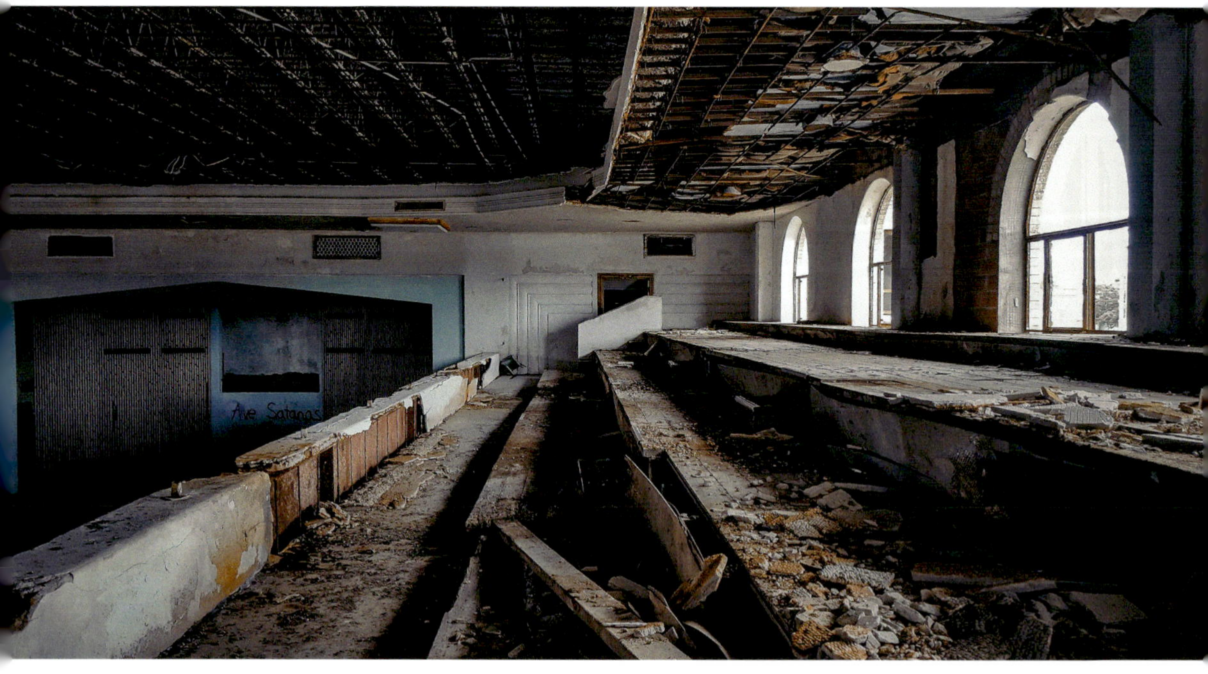

Damaged second-level stadium seating.

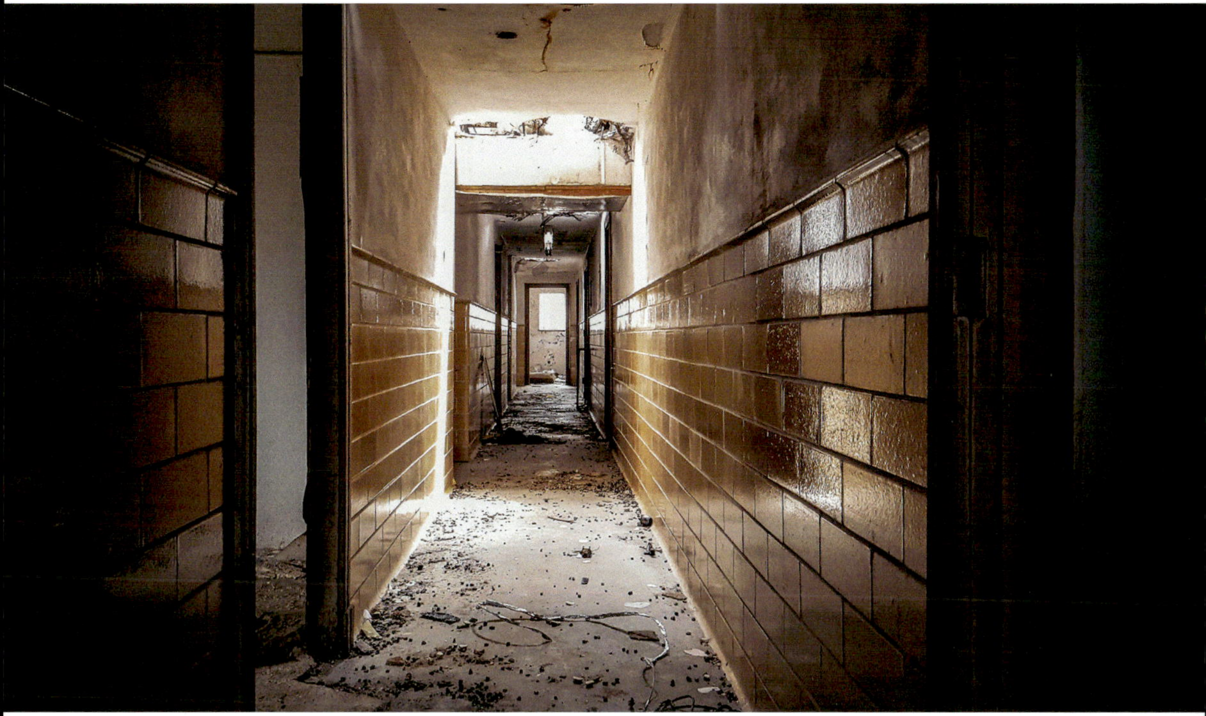

Yellow-tiled nostalgic hallway.

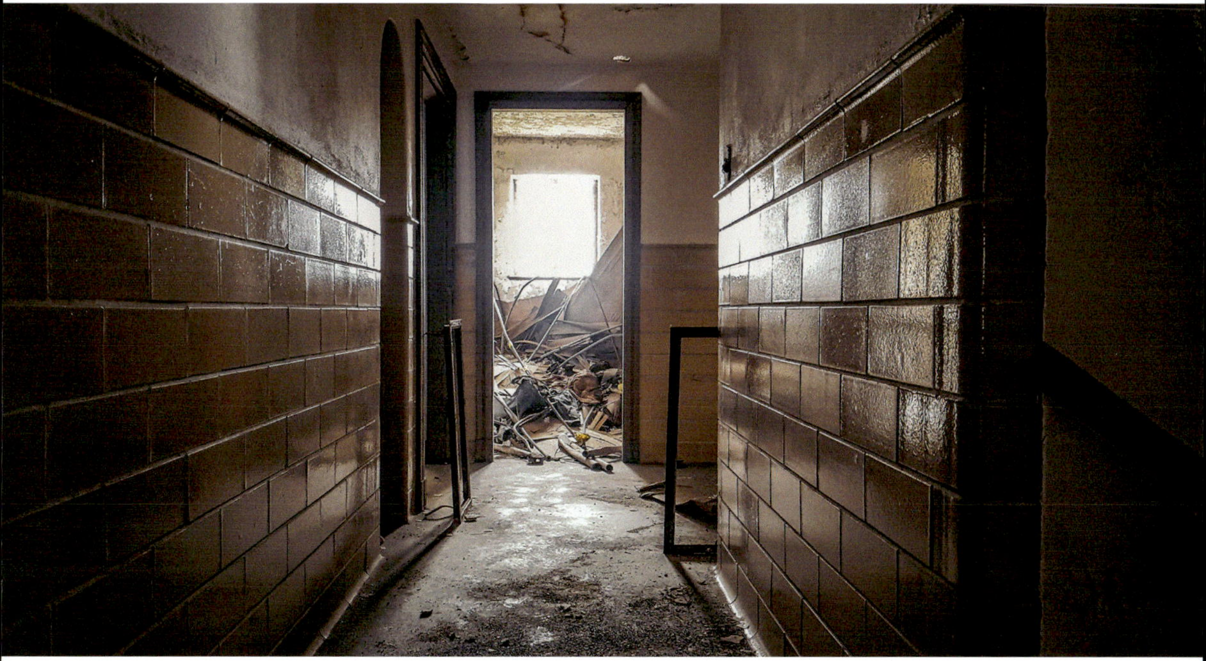

Tiled hallway with scrapped pipes.

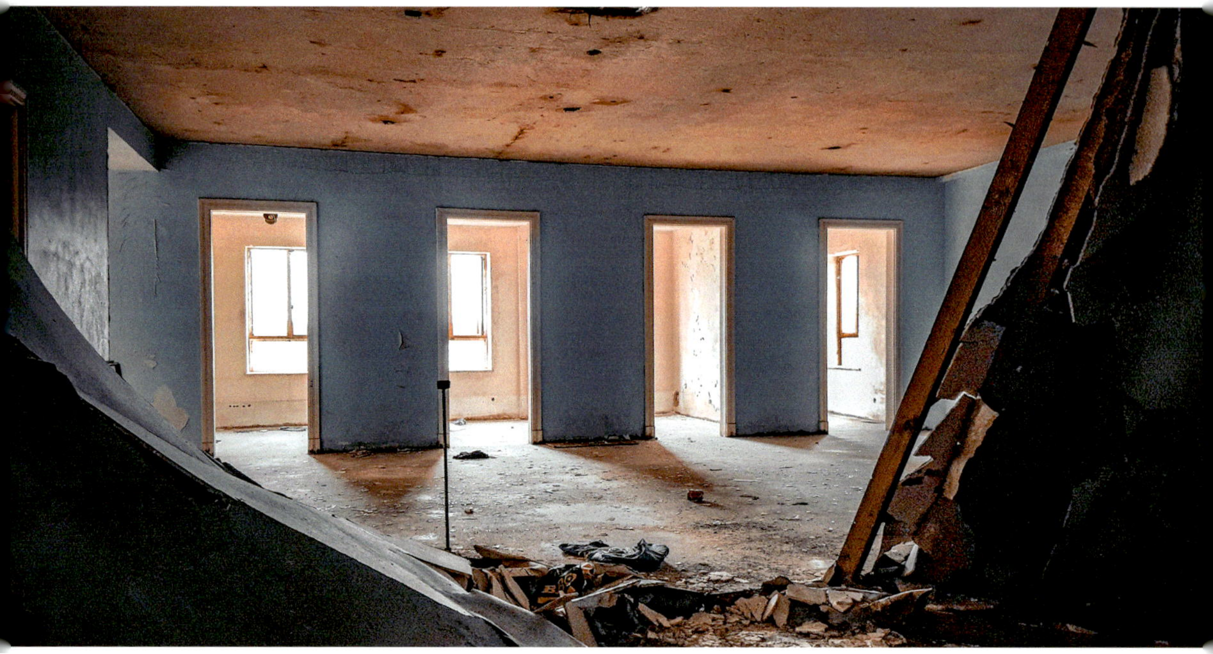

Light blue painted room.

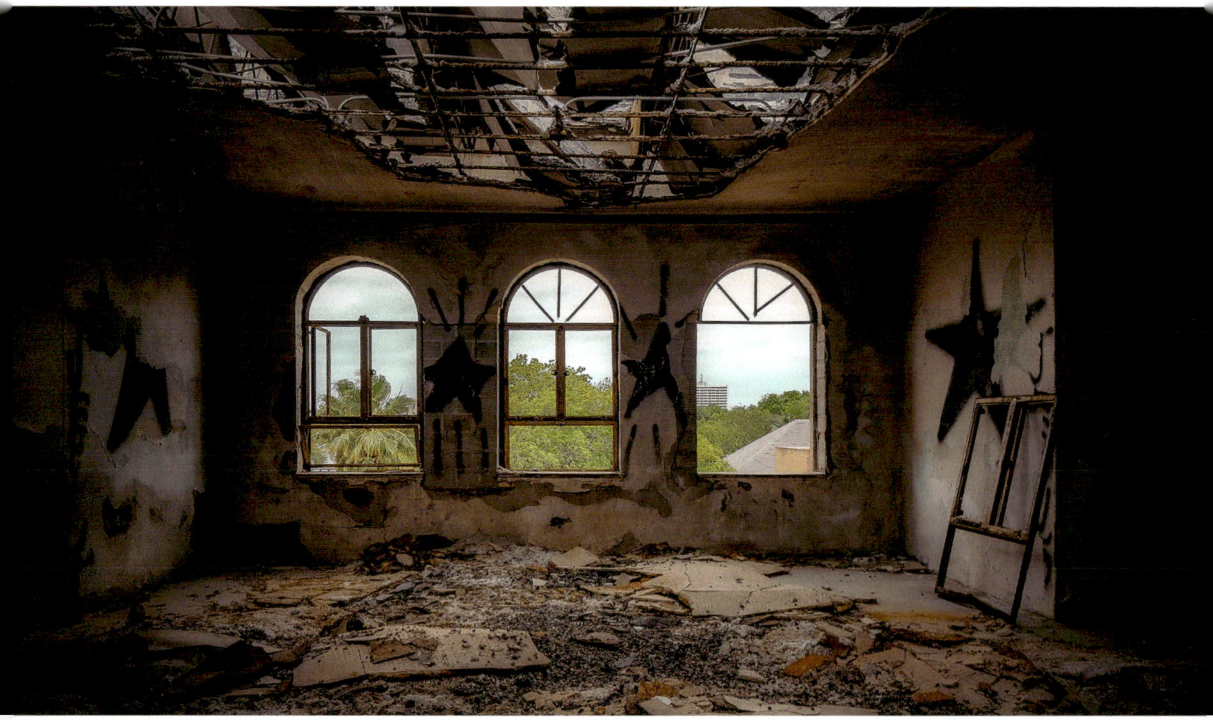

Three remaining arches.

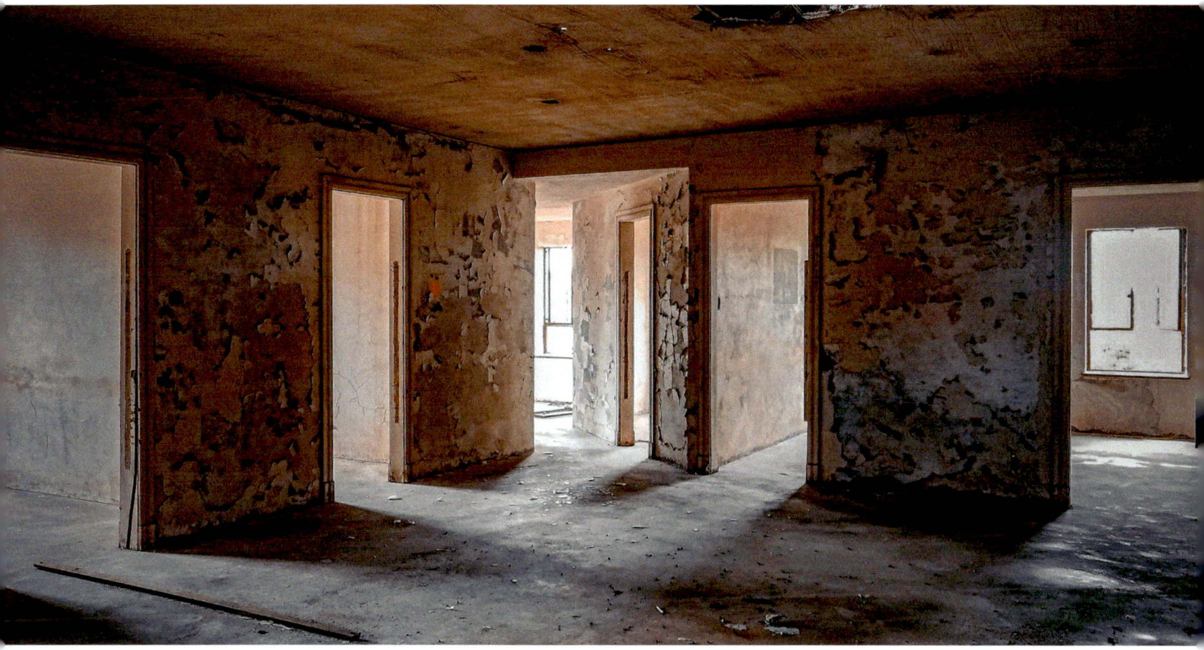

Open area with surrounding doors.

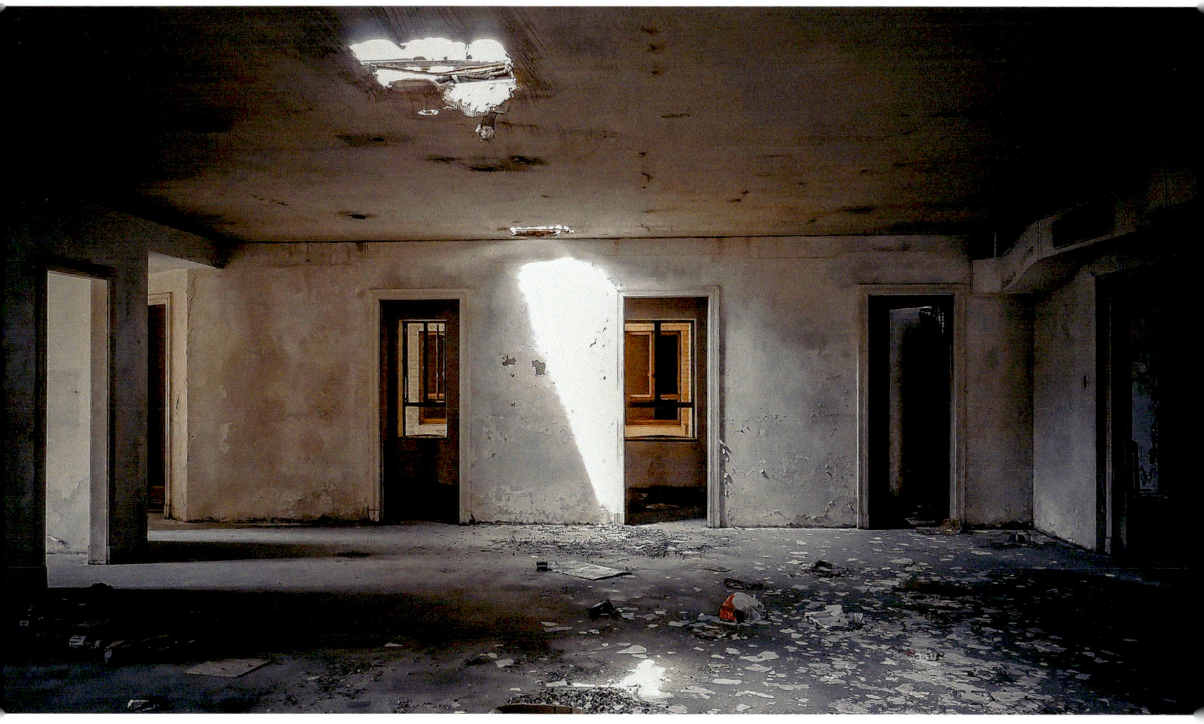

Complex layout hinting at school use.

During my exploration, I discovered a makeshift home hidden within the church's heart that spoke volumes about its inhabitants and the role this old building once played and was playing in that moment. Encountering a couple living there evoked a mix of fear, tension, and intrigue; their hostile demeanor reminded me that I was essentially trespassing in what they considered home. The irony was not lost on me—they were the original trespassers. Gentrification and revitalization had pushed them into this disregarded space, which to me, stressed the complex dynamics of displacement.

In October 2019, the church's final chapter began with its demolition, paving the way for an apartment complex. Uptown Corpus Christi's gentrification is progressing slowly, allowing city planners to engage with the community more effectively. Regular meetings help ensure development plans address local needs and support affordable housing and small businesses, minimizing displacement.

This gradual pace should serve to provide more time to develop affordable housing projects, protecting long-time residents from being priced out and preserving the neighborhood's diversity and character.

With more time, local businesses can receive support to adapt to changing economic conditions. Programs offering financial aid, business resources, and protections against sudden rent hikes can help small businesses stay open, preserving Uptown Corpus Christi's unique character.

Gentrification is widespread across Texas and the U.S., affecting cities from Houston to Austin to San Antonio. Like Corpus Christi, these cities face the challenge of balancing economic development with cultural displacement. By learning from each other's experiences, cities can pursue inclusive planning that nurtures growth while maintaining their unique identities.

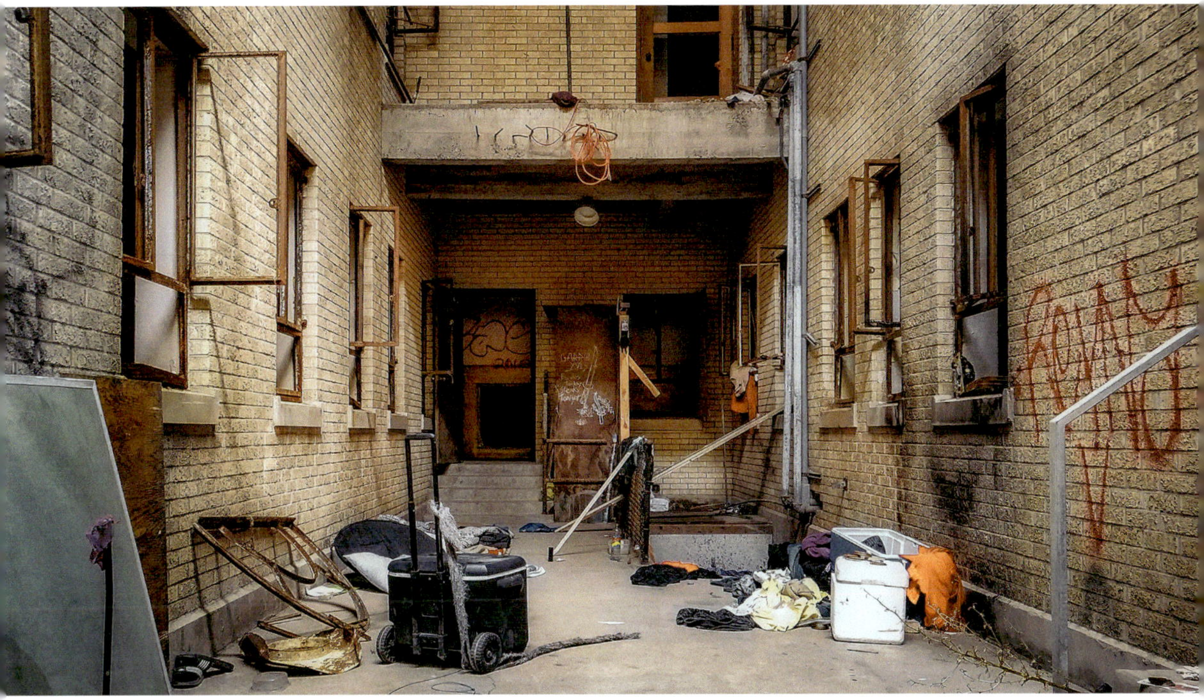

Squatters' quarters on ground level.

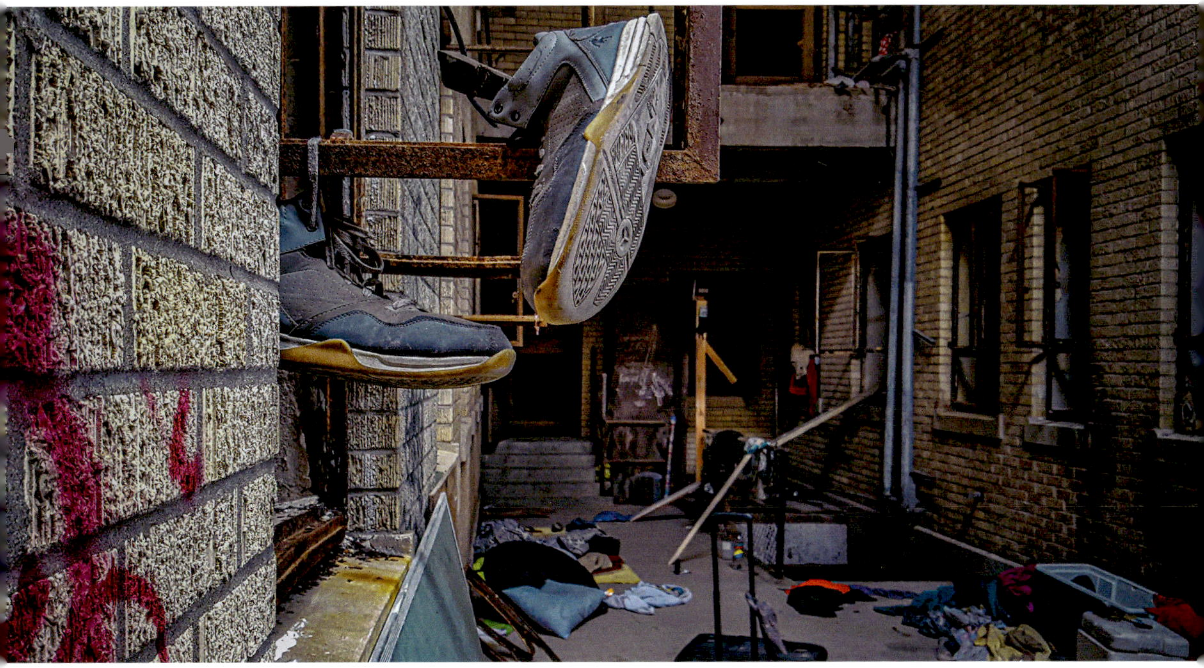

Close-up of squatters' living space.

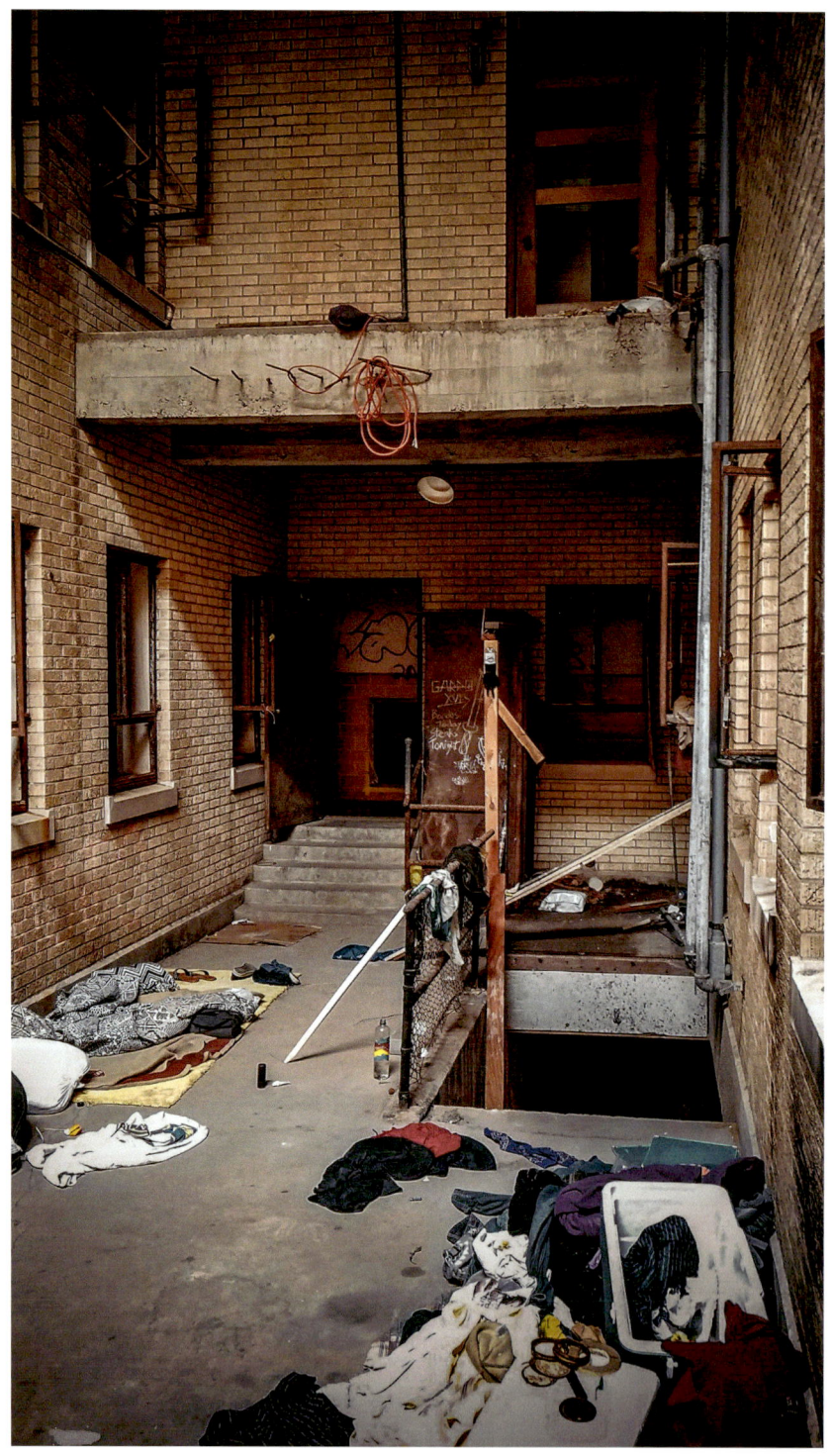

Windows overlooking open-air space.

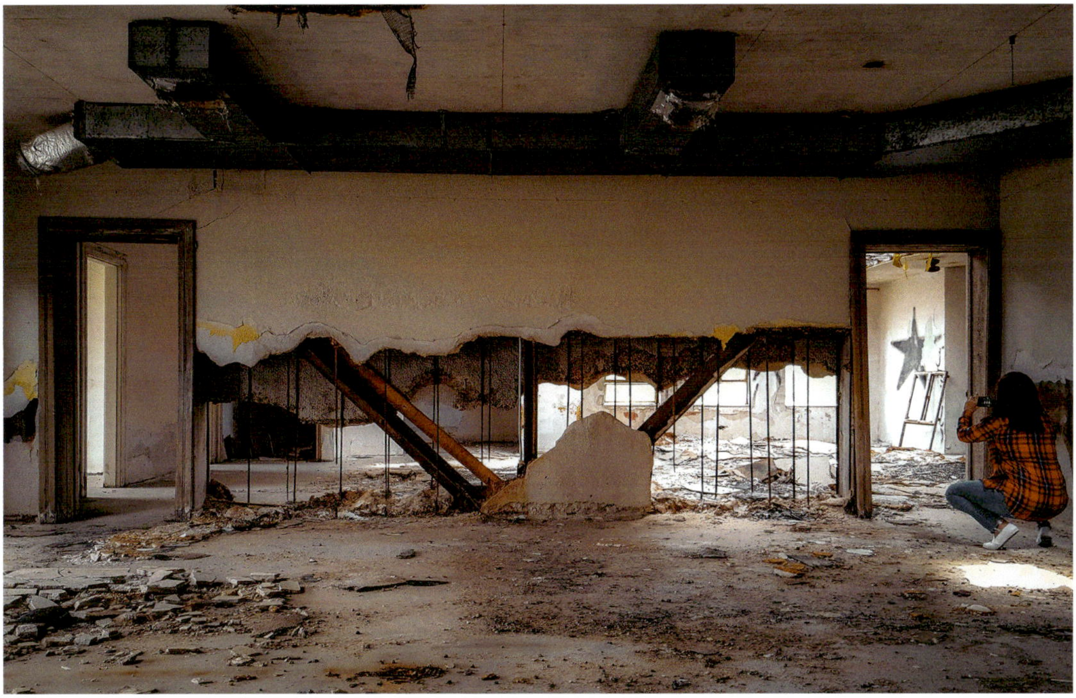

Scrapped walls exposing metal.

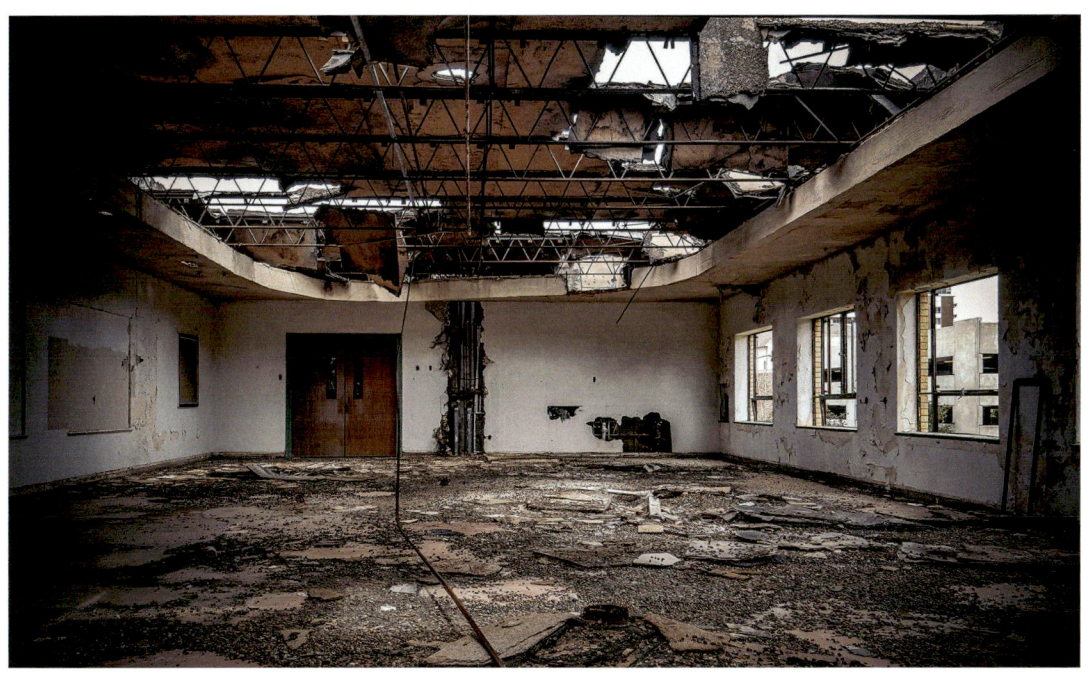

Ballroom entrance view.

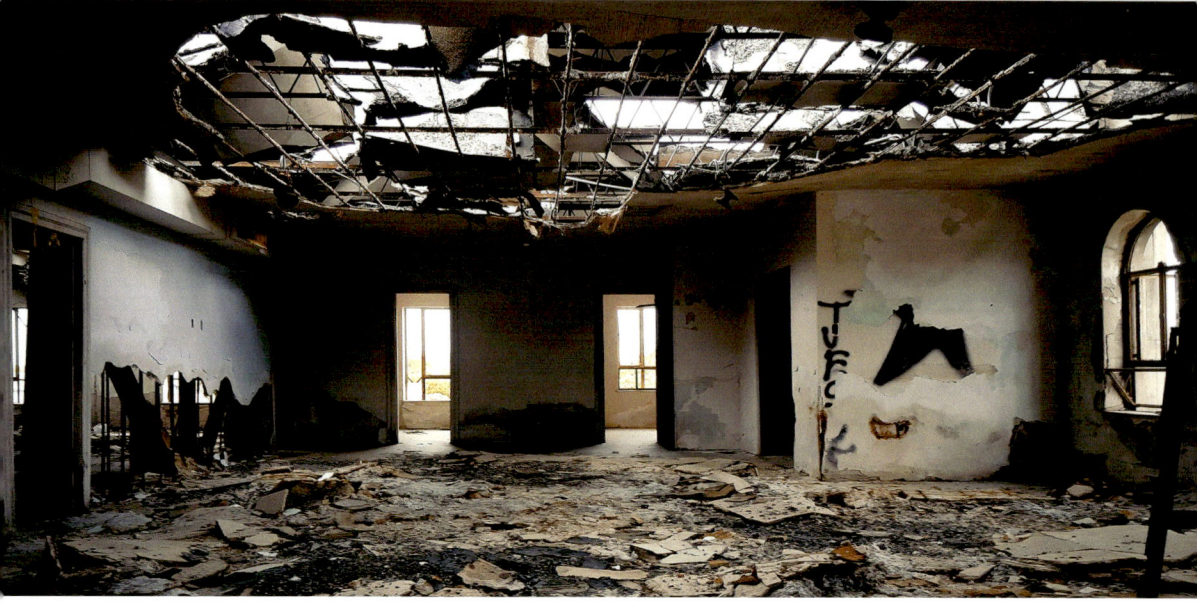

Open area showing severe decay.

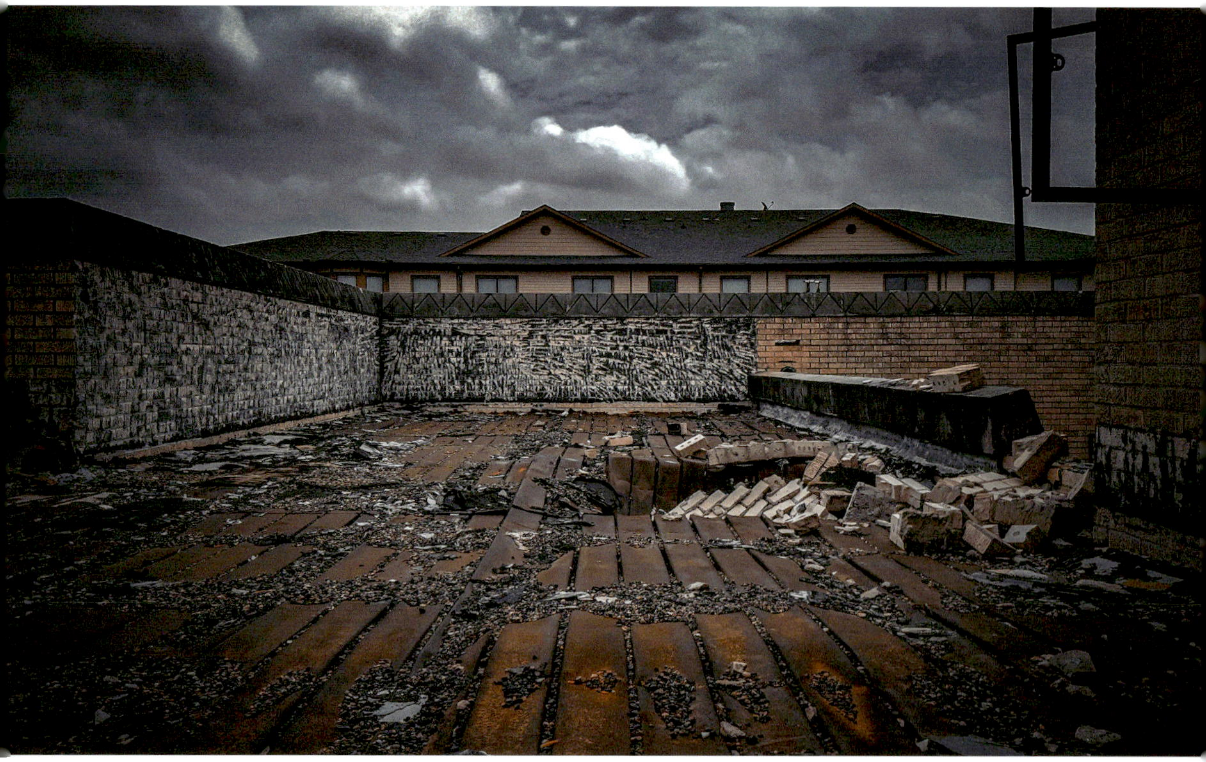

Rooftop gathering area in disrepair.

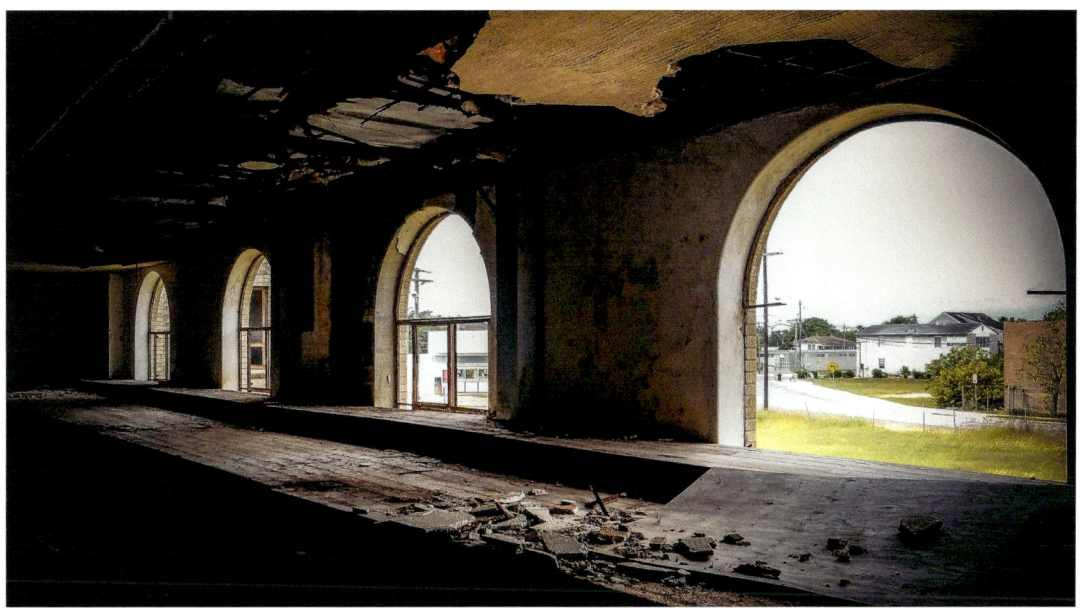

Arched former ballroom or cafeteria.

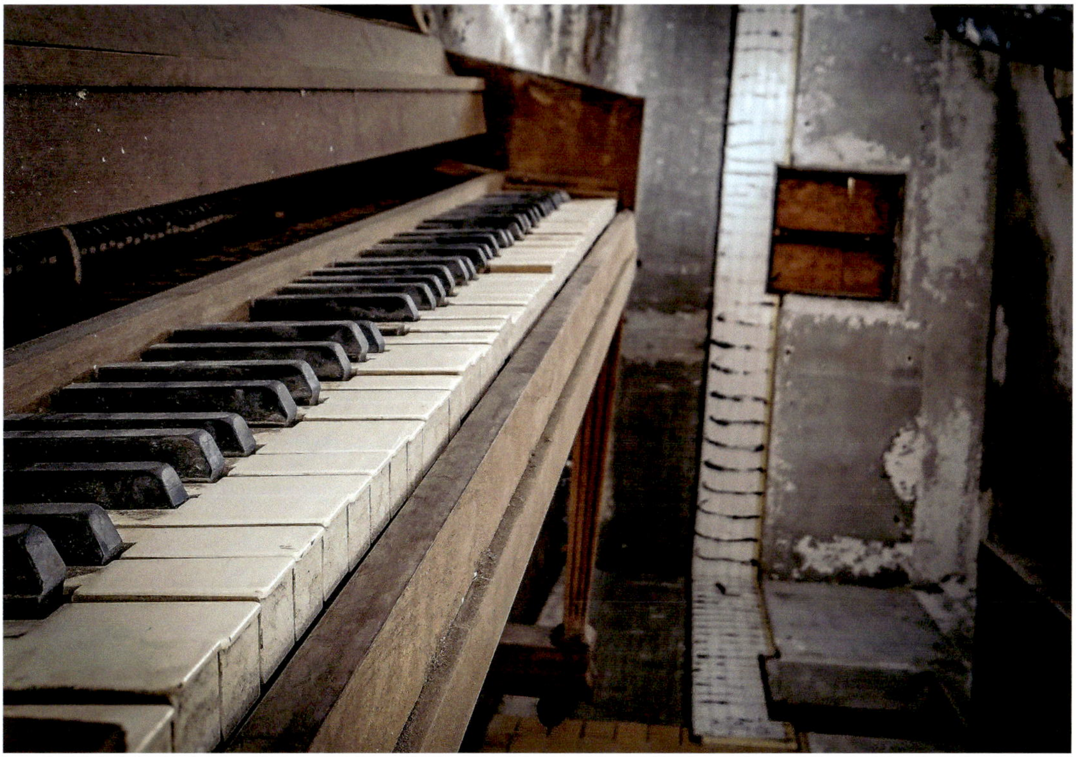

Decaying piano close-up.

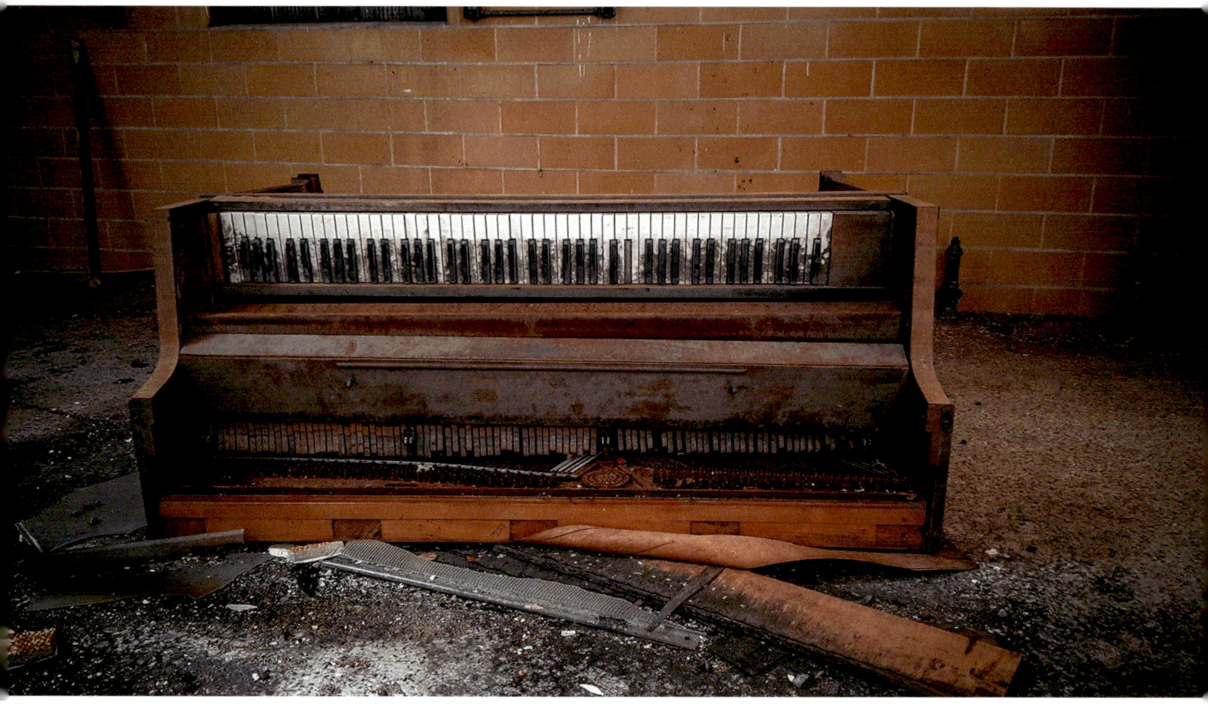

Lonely pianos left behind.

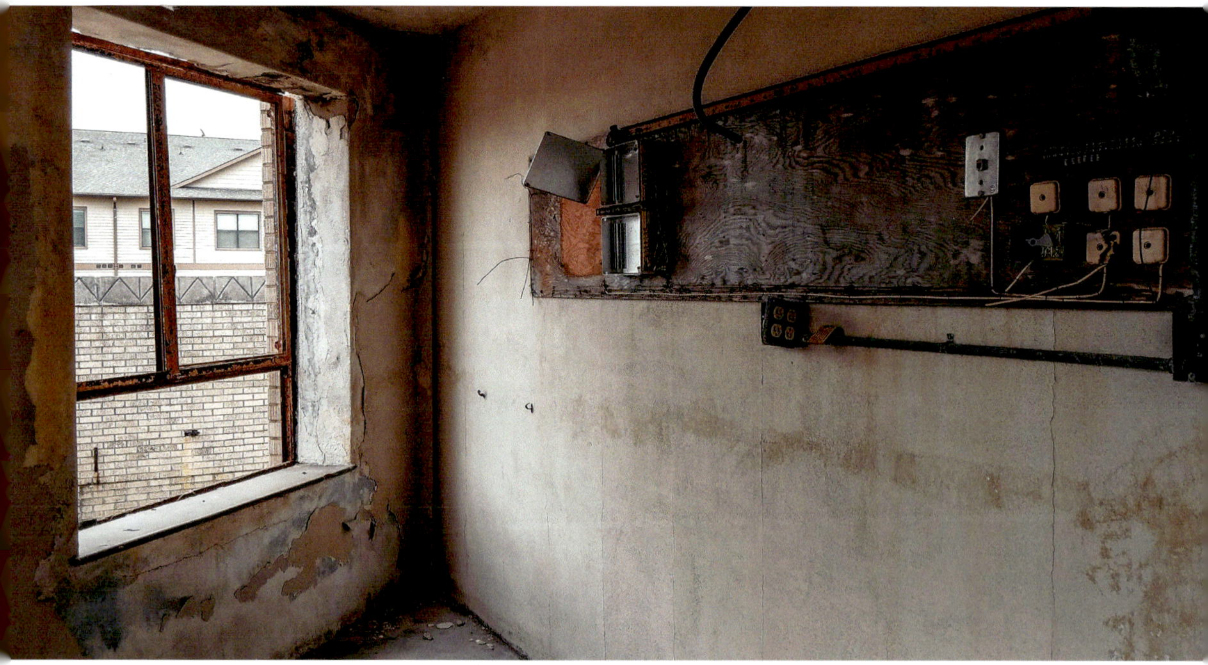

Stripped power panel.

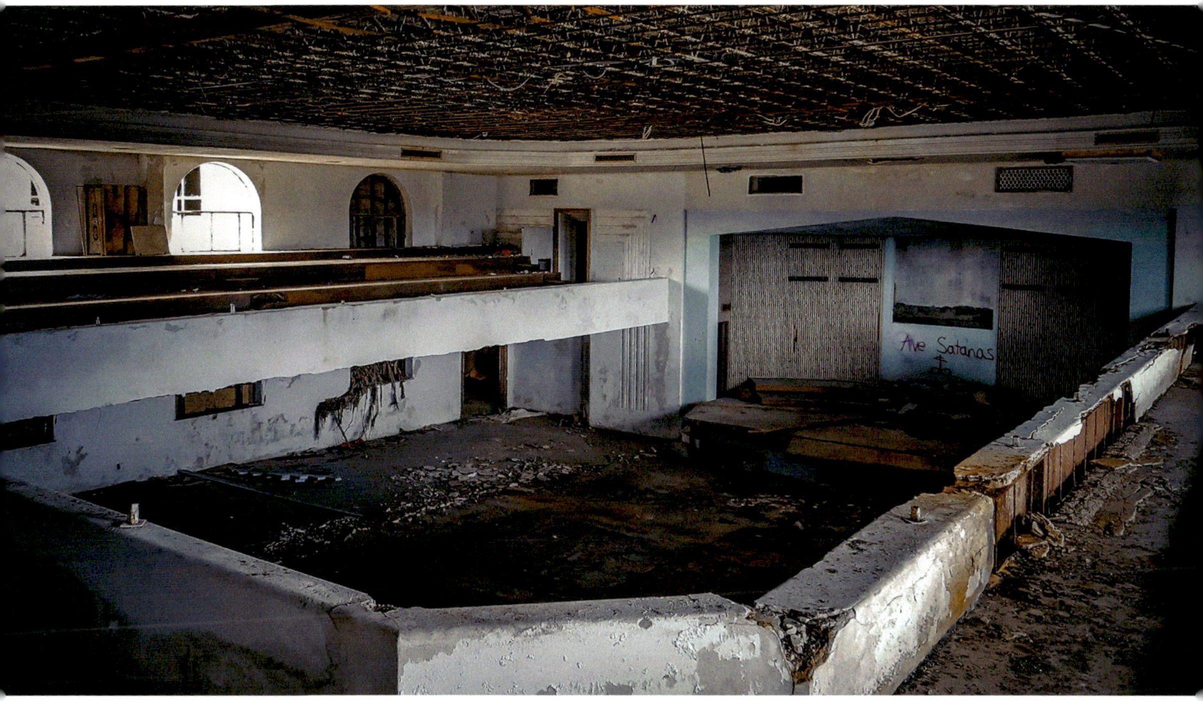

Wall designs down to the first floor.

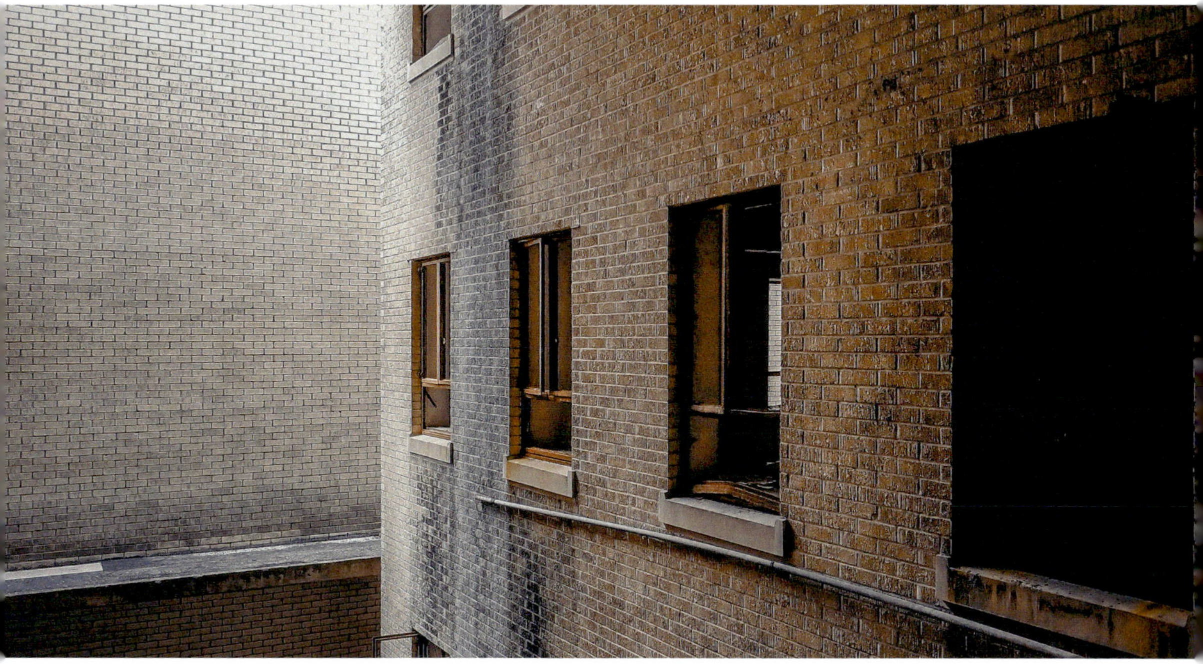

Properly spaced windows amid decay.

13

Bonus Content

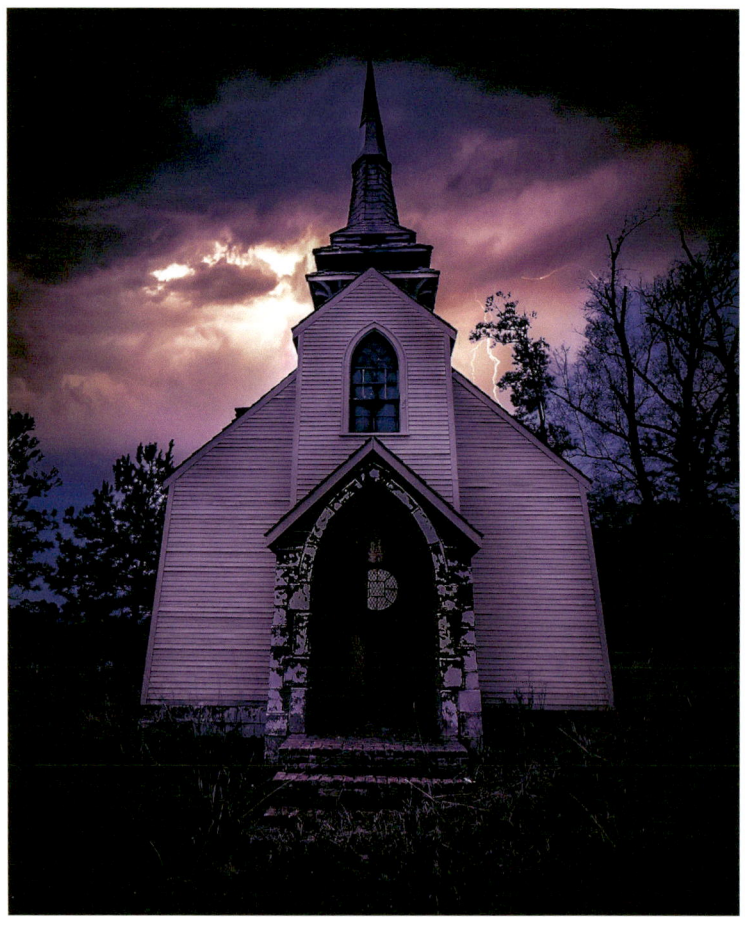

Low-angle exterior with tall steeple.

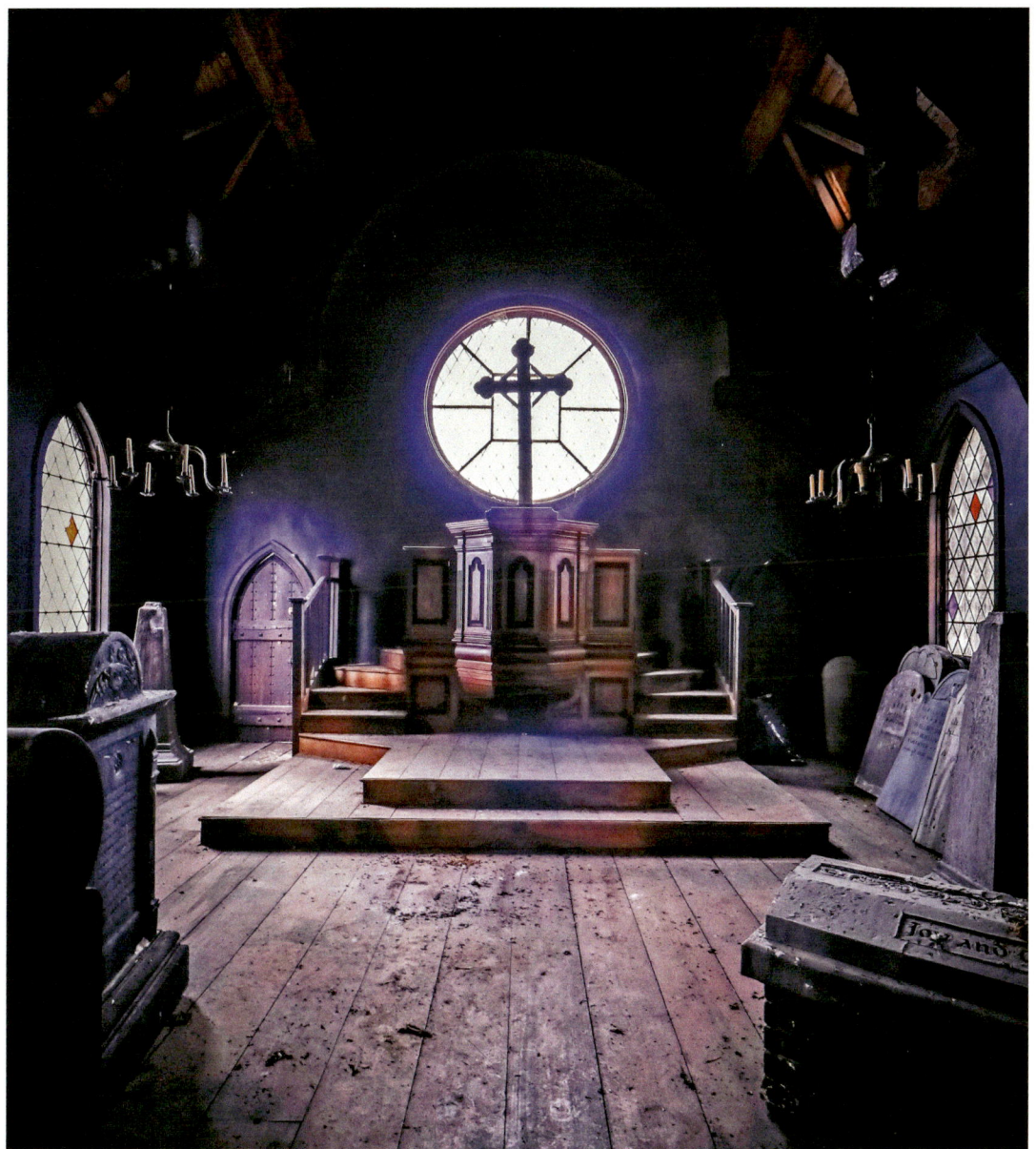

Altar view with centered cross.

Have you ever watched the series *Salem*? If so, these next photos might look familiar. While this building is not technically in Texas, and also technically not a church, it is close enough to the border and intriguing enough to include in this book. The images here are of the abandoned TV set used for the show, featuring the very church that appears in the series.

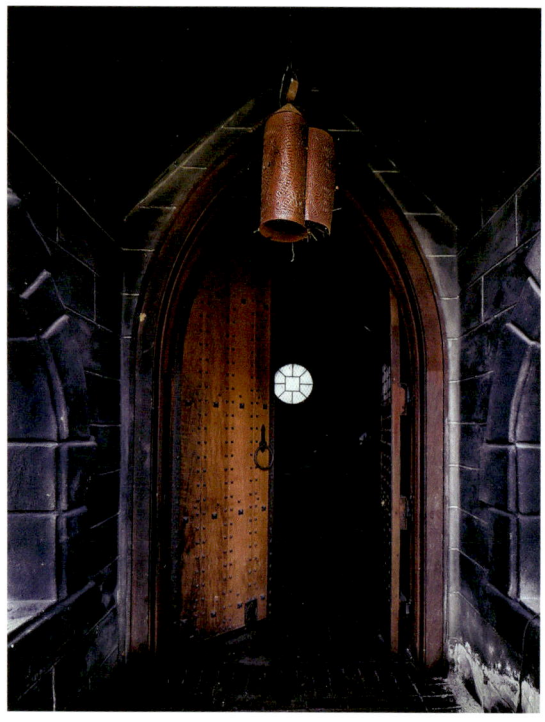

Left: Entrance with distinct light fixture.

Below left: Candlelit chandelier near stained glass.

Below right: Deteriorating chairs inside.

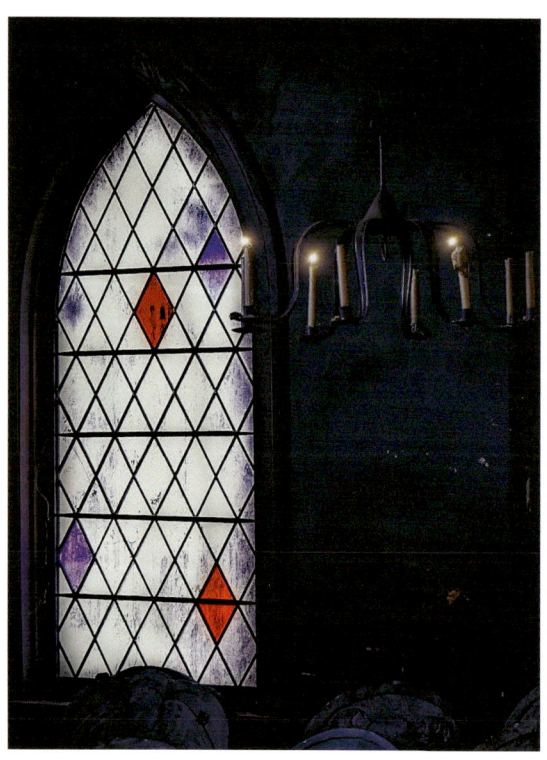

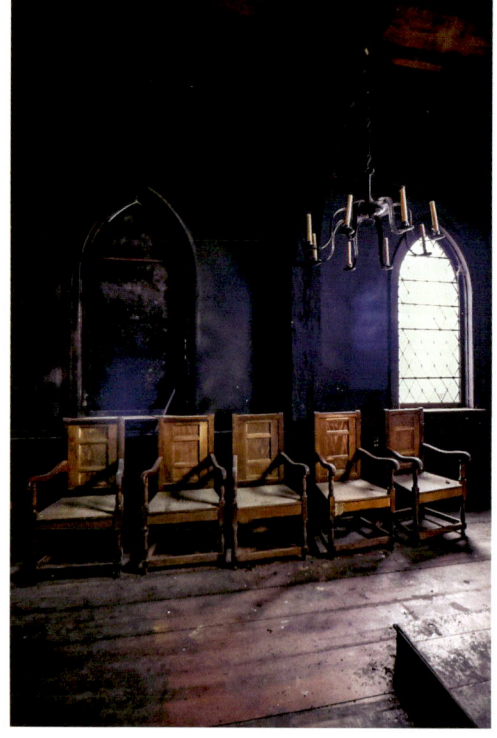

Conclusion

In exploring religion in Texas, our travels have taken us to the majestic structures and humble sanctuaries that once stood as beacons of hope, community, and faith.

As we witness the decline of these once-vibrant worship centers, we are reminded of the importance of preserving our cultural and religious heritage while carving a way for a healthier yet sustainable future. The efforts of communities to restore and repurpose these buildings are a testament to the resilience and creativity that define the Texan spirit. They inspire us to value and protect the legacy passed down through generations. The key to achieving this is balance and consideration of those who have been lifelong residents while understanding the needs of the future.

The forces of gentrification, redlining, and shifting political landscapes have shaped not only where people worship but also where they can live, work, and thrive. Government grants once used to establish settlements and institutions have not always been equally accessible, and even today, disparities persist. Religious institutions have been both sanctuaries and battlegrounds in the fight for civil rights, a reminder that faith and social justice are deeply intertwined.

Religion in Texas continues to evolve, making it a mosaic of traditions, each contributing to Texan culture. While challenges and conflicts persist, they offer opportunities for dialogue, understanding, and growth. If we truly wish to preserve these spaces, we must also preserve the histories of those who built them—their struggles, their triumphs, and the systemic barriers they faced. Only by acknowledging the past in its entirety can we build a future where faith remains a source of strength and unity. So, what steps will our nation take to ensure that history's darkest chapters are not repeated? And more importantly, will we have the courage to listen, learn, and act before history begins to repeat itself?

Bibliography

Cain, S., "Photos: Abandoned Texas Church Turned into One-Bedroom Rental Loft," *Business Insider*, www.businessinsider.com/photos-abandoned-texas-church-turned-into-one-bedroom-rental-loft-2024-2

Evans, S., "Jasper, Texas 20 Years After James Byrd Jr. Was Dragged to Death," *Business Insider*, www.businessinsider.com/jasper-texas-20-years-after-james-byrd-jr-was-dragged-to-death-2019-4

"Fire Destroys Recently Restored Bartlett Church That Had Stood Since 1890," FOX 7 Austin, www.fox7austin.com/news/fire-destroys-recently-restored-bartlett-church-that-had-stood-since-1890

Gross, T., "How Religion Turned Texas Red," *The Daily Beast*, www.thedailybeast.com/how-religion-turned-texas-red

"Guadalupe El Torero Church," Explore Texas Blog, exploretexas.blog/2016/06/17/guadalupe-el-torero-church/

"Historical Marker—Bartlett Presbyterian Church," Historical Marker Database, www.hmdb.org/m.asp?m=26048

"Historical Marker—Sharp Presbyterian Church," Historical Marker Database, www.hmdb.org/m.asp?m=117611

"Historical Plaque—Doucette," Open Plaques, openplaques.org/plaques/27325

"History of St. Joseph Catholic Church Rockdale," St. Joseph Catholic Church Rockdale, stjosephrockdale.org/about-us/history/

"*Jasper, Texas* (Film)," Wikipedia, en.wikipedia.org/wiki/Jasper,_Texas_(film)#:~:text=Jasper%2C%20Texas%20is%20a%202003,African%20American%20James%20Byrd%20Jr

"Jermyn, Texas," Wikipedia, en.wikipedia.org/wiki/Jermyn_Texas

Kim, P., "Historic Palestine Church Awarded $75,000 for Repairs," KLTV, January 20, 2023, www.kltv.com/2023/01/20/historic-palestine-church-awarded-75000-repairs/

"Mount Vernon African Methodist Episcopal Church (Palestine, Texas)," Wikipedia, en.wikipedia.org/wiki/Mount_Vernon_African_Methodist_Episcopal_Church_(Palestine,_Texas)

"Rivercrest Project Benefiting Unit Road System," KTRE, www.ktre.com/video/2021/11/13/rivercrest-project-benefiting-unit-road-system/

"Sharp, Texas," Texas Escapes, www.texasescapes.com/CentralTexasTownsSouth/Sharp-Texas.htm

"Special Report: Rivercrest Residents Describe the Lost Paradise," KTRE, www.ktre.com/story/11936208/special-report-rivercrest-residents-describe-the-lost-paradise/

Bibliography

Texas Almanac, "Religion in Early Texas," Texas Almanac, www.texasalmanac.com/articles/religion-in-early-texas

"Texas Historical Marker—Jermyn, Texas," Historical Marker Database, www.hmdb.org/m.asp?m=200142

Texas State Historical Association, "Bartlett, TX," Texas State Historical Association, www.tshaonline.org/handbook/entries/bartlett-tx

Texas State Historical Association, "Clarkson, TX," Texas State Historical Association, www.tshaonline.org/handbook/entries/clarkson-tx

Texas State Historical Association, "Doucette, TX," Texas State Historical Association, www.tshaonline.org/handbook/entries/doucette-tx

Texas State Historical Association, "Linn, TX," Texas State Historical Association, www.tshaonline.org/handbook/entries/linn-tx

Texas State Historical Association, "Religion," Texas State Historical Association, www.tshaonline.org/handbook/entries/religion

Texas State Historical Association, "Rockdale, TX," Texas State Historical Association, www.tshaonline.org/handbook/entries/rockdale-tx

"The Bartlett First Presbyterian Church: Before and After," Bartlett Secrets, bartlettsecrets.com/2022/09/the-bartlett-first-presbyterian-church-before-and-after/

"Uptown Corridors—Revitalization Strategy," Archive.org, archive.org/details/cicctx-Uptown_Corridors_-_Revitalization_Strategy_-_Staples_and_Leopard

About the Author

I am a Texas-based realtor with a passion for helping individuals and families secure their futures through homeownership. Yet my passion extends beyond real estate. I believe in using my success in the industry to uplift and empower underprivileged communities, providing opportunities for stability, education, and generational wealth.

Yet, my work in real estate is just the beginning. I believe that homeownership is more than just a financial investment—it's a foundation for stability and success. That's why I am building The Bright Nest Foundation—this initiative will be dedicated to providing housing support, educational resources, and community development opportunities for those who need it most. My journey has been shaped by a love for photography, a deep respect for history, and a drive to create meaningful change. From exploring forgotten spaces in Texas to capturing untold stories, I have always sought to uncover not just what is, but what could be. That same mindset fuels my approach to real estate—helping my clients find not just a house, but a home where they can build their futures.

I am dedicated not only to your real estate success but also to empowering communities and creating real change

Adriana Perez
409.927.0881
www.thetrochilidae.com

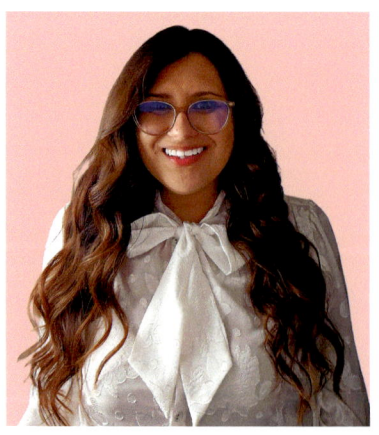